AUTHENTIC

AUTHENTIC

AUTHENTIC

The Bible — an authentic book

Brian H Edwards

To Rosie,
for her continued love,
encouragement and
strong prayerful support

© Day One Publications 2015

ISBN 978-1-84625-465-9

All Scripture quotations, unless stated otherwise, are from The Holy Bible, New International Version Copyright © 1973, 1978, 1984 International Bible Society

British Library Cataloguing in Publication Data available

Published by Day One Publications
Ryelands Road, Leominster, HR6 8NZ
Telephone 01568 613 740   Fax 01568 611 473
North America Toll Free 888 329 6630
email—sales@dayone.co.uk
web site—www.dayone.co.uk

Cover design by smallprint
Printed by T J International

2 The Bible — an authentic book

Contents

Introduction: The Bible is an authentic book

Why should we bother to read the Bible?

Half a million words recounting the history of two million people who, three thousand years ago, occupied a small plot of land measuring around one hundred and thirty miles by forty, in a seemingly unremarkable part of the world: it sounds as if it is hardly the stuff to fascinate the twenty-first-century reader.

On the other hand, there is something about the Bible that immediately strikes us as significant.

The Bible was written by approximately forty different writers over a period of at least fifteen hundred years; some lived during the mysterious Egyptian civilizations and others under the cruel Assyrians, the powerful Babylonians, the staggeringly wealthy Persians or the well ordered Romans. Some writers were kings or courtiers, others were priests or prophets, farmers or fishermen, civil servants or soldiers. These facts alone are sufficient for us to make the claim that the Bible is a unique book. However, being unique does not make it necessarily important.

What is even more amazing to discover is that, given the long period of time over which it was written and the longer period of history that it covers, the Bible is not a random collection of ancient books about God, but there is a plan—a big story—that is clearly progressing as you read on. One of the exciting things about reading the Bible is to watch how each book and chapter fits together into the great overall theme.

Unlike all other sacred texts of the world religions, the Christian Bible is embedded in history, and this history is found in almost every book. The narrative of Israel throughout the Old Testament, the life of Jesus Christ in the four Gospels, the record of the early Christian church in the book of Acts, and the letters of the apostles to the Christian congregations across the widespread Roman Empire all contain details, references and allusions to actual events, places and people.

The Bible is packed with specifics of what actually happened, and these frequently fit times, places, events and people known to us from sources outside the Bible. This means that we can check out the record and verify its claims. While the Christian accepts the accuracy of the Bible by faith, it is not faith at the expense of intelligent understanding. The more we discover of the Bible in its context, the more we become aware of just how accurate its historical record is.

The eminent Ulster literary critic C. S. Lewis once wrote, 'The first qualification for judging any piece of workmanship, from a corkscrew to a cathedral, is to know what it is—what it was intended to do and how it is meant to be used.'[1] If we apply that to the Bible, we will not judge it by what *we* think it is meant to be, but by what it claims to be.

God's big story

A few years ago, Professor Richard Dawkins at the University of Oxford published his assessment of the Bible:

To be fair, the Bible is not systematically evil but just plain weird, as you would expect of a chaotically cobbled-together anthology of disjointed documents, composed, revised, translated, distorted and 'improved' by hundreds of anonymous authors, editors and copyists, unknown to us and mostly unknown to each other, spanning nine centuries.[2]

It is difficult to imagine a more thoughtless and superficial statement than this. It is admittedly a catchy sound bite, for which Dawkins is fairly accomplished, but it reveals a shallow reading of the text of the Bible, an

---

1 C. S. Lewis, *A Preface to Paradise Lost* (Oxford / New York: Oxford University Press, 1942), p. 1.
2 Richard Dawkins, *The God Delusion* (London, Transworld Publishers (Bantam Press), 2006), p. 237.

unawareness of the formation and transmission of the Bible, and a total ignorance of its message. If half of his assessment was true, it is astounding that millions of ordinary readers and Christian scholars over the past two thousand years have found such a coherent and unfolding message throughout its pages.

The Bible is unique among all books ever written over the course of human history, whether sacred or secular, not only because of the composite of authors over such a long period, but because it has a consistent message throughout. Far from being 'chaotically cobbled-together' it is a perfect mosaic revealing God's purposes and plans for the human race—something that most junior-grade children can grasp.

The narrative of the Bible goes like this:

It begins with the account of God's creation of the universe, including Planet Earth and the human race. Then follows the tragic episode of rebellion against God's perfect commands, and the inevitable downward spiral of suffering and violence that followed. However, at the outset, in Genesis 3:15, God gave a promise that one day a deliverer would come who would crush the great enemy and deceiver of the human race, the devil. This was God's great promise, the fulfilment of which runs as an unbroken thread throughout the remainder of the Old Testament.

God chose a nation, Israel, through which he would eventually carry out his promise. The first five books of the Bible trace the emergence of this nation and the constant, underlying focus on the family line that would lead to this rescuer, known as the Messiah. Much of the history of Israel throughout the remainder of the Old Testament, and written against the background of the pagan nations surrounding it, reveals God protecting his chosen people in order to guard the family line of the Messiah. Some of the narratives—such as the escape from Egypt recorded in the book of Exodus, the story of a refugee in a foreign land in the tiny book of Ruth, and the account of a Jewish queen in the Persian court in the book of Esther—all reinforce the fact that God can and will look after his people whenever and wherever they are.

Throughout the whole of the Old Testament God sent his prophets, who encouraged or challenged the chosen nation. Those prophets who have books named after them, such as Isaiah, Jeremiah, Ezekiel and Daniel—there are seventeen in all—fit perfectly into the historical narrative. But at the same time each of them was pointing ever more clearly to the coming of the Messiah. Even the casual reader of the Bible can discover many passages where the promise is of someone who will come to deliver God's people from the power of the devil (see the 'Outline of the Old Testament' in Part 3, page 103).

Finally, as Paul in the New Testament expressed it so simply, 'When the time had fully come, God sent his Son, born of a woman, born under law, to redeem those under law, that we might receive the full rights of sons' (Gal. 4:4). The birth, life, death and resurrection of Jesus Christ were the fulfilment of the great promise given by God when the human race rebelled against his authority and brought misery upon itself. In other words, the entire narrative of the Old Testament is a preparation for the coming of Jesus Christ into the world. By his perfect life, and his death and resurrection, he destroyed the ultimate power of the devil and promised all who will trust in him reconciliation with God and eternal life in new heavens and a new earth.

That is God's big story. And the evidence that all the New Testament writers understood the Old Testament as a preparation for the coming of Christ is seen in the fact that in 528 verses of the New Testament there are 419 exact quotations from the Old. In addition there are hundreds more allusions to passages in the Old Testament.

Of course there are parts of the Bible that are hard to understand, and there are severe judgements upon people and nations that need to be understood against the background of the unbelievable brutality and immorality of Israel's surrounding nations; but God's big story unfolds progressively and with more clarity as the history of Israel develops.

However, the Bible is much more than just a preparation for the coming of Christ; it is a revelation of the character of God himself. In contrast to all the false idols of the nations surrounding Israel, God revealed himself as a moral God who expected a high standard of morality from his people. By his life and teaching, and expounded further by the apostles in the New Testament letters, Jesus Christ has given us the highest moral standard this world will ever see. For two millennia Christians who have been reading their Bible and conforming their lives according to its teaching have set the world an example of honesty, integrity, diligent hard work, and a charitable care of those in need. The legacy of those who follow the example of Christ far outweighs anything that can be offered by the combined contributions of the world religions and atheism.

The purpose of all that follows here is to show that God's big story is revealed to us within a book that is reliable, and that this is evidenced by the authentic nature of the writing. It is not the purpose here to resolve all the 'hard parts' of the Bible—many commentators have adequately tackled these over the years—but to show that the Bible reveals itself as true and accurate, reliable and trustworthy.

The evidence of witnesses

Simon Greenleaf (1783–1853), one of the founders of Harvard Law School, set out to disprove the resurrection of Jesus Christ. In the event, like others after him, he was persuaded that the Gospel records were authentic eyewitness accounts of the most momentous life, death and resurrection in human history. This led him to expand his approach and set down a number of qualifications for any honest study of the Scriptures.[3]

Greenleaf insisted that approaching the Bible does not mean 'the surrender of the reason and judgement', but it does mean a willingness to pursue impartially and to weigh the arguments and evidence as far as possible without prejudice or hostility. Our approach to the Bible is, he continued, 'a subject fraught with such momentous consequences to man'. If the Bible is what it claims to be—the wholly reliable word of God—and if Jesus Christ is who he claims to be—the perfect and eternal Son of God—then any study of the Bible must be undertaken with humility and a sincere desire to come to a knowledge of the truth.

---

3 Simon Greenleaf, *Testimony of the Evangelists* (1846; repr. of 1874 edition: Grand Rapids: Baker, 1984). This was the result of his three-volume *Treatise on the Law of Evidence*, 1842–1853.

The lawyer set out what our starting position on the Bible should be. He summarized it like this:

That the books of the Old Testament, as we now have them, are genuine; that they existed in the time of our Saviour, and were commonly received and referred to among the Jews as the sacred books of their religion; and that the text of the Four Evangelists has been handed down to us in the state in which it was originally written, that is, without having been materially corrupted or falsified, either by heretics or Christians. These are facts which we are entitled to assume as true until the contrary is shown.

He then followed this with a number of universally accepted legal principles which, he claimed, ought always to be applied to the biblical record. The following is a summary:

- Documents, ancient or modern, have the right to be taken as a true and correct record unless and until proven otherwise: 'In trials of fact, by oral testimony, the proper inquiry is not whether it is possible that the testimony may be false, but whether there is sufficient probability that it is true.'

- The character of the author of a document is to be considered trustworthy unless or until it is proven otherwise. A witness is presumed credible until the contrary is shown.

- The number of independent witnesses confirms the greater likelihood of the accuracy of their report. And the agreement of their evidence significantly enhances the truth of their record.

- The reliability of a report is confirmed by the degree to which details match known events and circumstances.

The co-founder of Harvard Law School claimed that these principles, accepted in any impartial court of law, should always be applied when we approach the books of the Bible: 'To follow the truth wherever it may lead us.' He then applied this to the four Gospel writers.

If Matthew was the author of the first Gospel, he was employed in the highly complex Roman taxation system; he would have been well educated and 'an experienced and intelligent observer' needing to be familiar with all forms of 'fraud, imposture, cunning and deception', and therefore would have been careful to scrutinize all the information that came to him to make up his Gospel record. Apart from this he was an eyewitness of all that he wrote.

According to the earliest evidence, Mark wrote his Gospel under the direction of Peter, and was himself well acquainted with the apostles.[4] Luke, a clinical physician by profession, has been shown (and even more since Greenleaf's day) to have been a remarkably accurate historian.[5] John, like Matthew, was one of the twelve disciples of Christ and one of the three in the inner circle of his companions.

We have every right to accept that these were men of integrity and honesty unless the contrary is proven. Their wide agreement of detail adds to the authenticity of their work, and the 'apparent' discrepancies give us confidence in the independency of their accounts.

The conclusion is that our business is that of a lawyer 'examining the testimony of witnesses by the rules of his profession, in order to ascertain whether, if they had thus testified on oath, in a court of law, they would be entitled to credit, and whether their narratives, as we now have them, would be received as ancient documents coming from the proper custody'.

It is interesting how often historians are willing to accept the trustworthiness of writers from the ancient world and yet assume the inaccuracy of the biblical records. For example, Manetho and his *Aegyptiaca*, Caesar and his *Gallic Wars* and Josephus and his *History of the Jews* are each allowed the presumption of truth until they are found to be in error. The default position is always to allow them accuracy unless proved inaccurate. This default is frequently reversed when it comes to the biblical writers.

4　The church leader Papias (AD 69–135) made this claim in *From the Exposition of the Oracles of the Lord*, ch. 6, and quoted by Eusebius in *Ecclesiastical History* 16.
5　See especially the work of Sir William Mitchell Ramsay in *The Bearing of Recent Discovery on the Trustworthiness of the New Testament* (London: Hodder & Stoughton, 1914). And below on page 38.

In our own day, Professor Alan Millard is as well qualified as any to make a positive judgement regarding the Old Testament.[6] Millard underlines the importance of understanding the care with which ancient scribes, both pagan and Jewish, copied and re-copied the material in front of them. While it is always possible that some errors of transcription have crept into the text, Millard rightly concludes, 'The text we receive from antiquity has primacy over our ideas of what it ought to say.'

Millard draws a parallel between the transmission of the Hebrew text of the Old Testament and that of Babylonian texts of the same period. While we do not have many ancient copies of the Hebrew text to compare with the later copies, we do have evidence of the transmission of Babylonian texts. A prayer to the goddess Ishtar found in a Neo-Babylonian copy dated to around 600 BC was found to be an exact copy of one dated around 1400 BC and 'other works written out about 1600 BC were still being copied in the seventh century with little change'. While this careful accuracy is not always adhered to, it is evident that when scribes in the ancient world were motivated by the significance of their text, they were careful to copy without error.

Commenting on the text of the book of Esther, Professor Edwin Yamauchi notes the care of the Hebrew scribes even in the detail of the accurate spelling of foreign names, which can be paralleled to Persian texts of the same period. [7]

We know for certain that the Jewish scribes considered their Scriptures to be a most sacred text and that transcribing them was not only a hallowed duty but an awesome responsibility. The idea of the scribes copying in a careless manner and allowing numerous errors and changes to creep into the text is contrary to everything we know of the scrupulous care of Jewish scribes.

Millard wisely comments that 'in reading any text it is a grave matter to state the presence of an error without positive proof. Frequently the text in question will be the only source of evidence and so if it is "corrected"

---

6 Alan R. Millard, 'Approaching the Old Testament', *Themelios* (January 1977), pp. 34–39..
7 Edwin M. Yamauchi, *Persia and the Bible* (Grand Rapids: Baker, 1996), p. 238.

or treated with suspicion, the evidence is destroyed or adulterated with speculation.' In other words, as Greenleaf had demanded for the New Testament, a statement has the right to be accepted as true unless or until positive evidence can disprove it.

A simple example of this is seen when two scholars suggest that the details of 'Josiah's teenage religious awakening' recorded in 2 Chronicles 34:3 'are almost certainly biographical idealizations after-the-fact'. They are simply imposing upon the text their own preconceived ideas without a shadow of evidence and then presenting them as 'almost certainly'.[8]

---

8   Israel Finkelstein and Neil Asher Silberman, *The Bible Unearthed: Archaeology's New Vision of Ancient Israel and the Origin of Its Sacred Text* (New York: Touchstone, 2002), p. 275.

Part 1
The Authentic
New Testament

This is the disciple who testifies to these things and who wrote them down. We know that his testimony is true. Jesus did many other things as well. If every one of them were written down, I suppose that even the whole world would not have room for the books that would be written (John 21:24–25).

There are two claims here: first, that the records in John's Gospel are a true and accurate account of the life, death and resurrection of Jesus Christ; and, second, that there is much more of the three years of Jesus' public ministry that we are not told. Possibly we have recorded no more than a thousandth part of his teaching and actions.[1]

John's claim reflects the Christian lyric originally scribbled on the wall of an asylum:

Could we with ink the ocean fill,
And were the skies of parchment made,
Were every stalk on earth a quill,
And every man a scribe by trade,
To write the love of God above
Would drain the ocean dry.
Nor could the scroll contain the whole,
Though stretched from sky to sky.[2]

---

1 The eighteenth-century Methodist evangelist John Wesley regularly preached fifteen sermons a week. According to his busyness recorded in the Gospels, it is unlikely that Jesus taught for much less than twenty hours a week. If so, and if he spoke at the normal lecture speed of 130 words a minute, in three years he would have uttered in excess of 24,000,000 words. We have only 24,000 recorded in the Gospels, and much of that is repeated.

It is a time-worn theory that most of the New Testament was not written until well into the second century at the earliest. However, in 1976 Bishop John A. T. Robinson, a liberal New Testament scholar, published *Redating the New Testament*, in which he concluded that the entire New Testament was complete before AD 70.[3] Robinson supported this with arguments from a careful study of every New Testament book, but especially from the fact that there is not one mention of what he called 'the single most datable and climactic event of the period', namely, the destruction of Jerusalem by the Roman army in AD 70.

What is even more significant about this book is the way Robinson criticized his fellow liberal scholars: 'Datings that seem agreed in the textbooks can suddenly appear much less secure than the consensus would suggest.'[4] 'It is astonishing that so much has continued to be built upon so little.'[5] He wrote of 'circular arguments' and 'presuppositions',[6] and deplored what he called 'disconcertingly tenuous deductions', 'sheer scholarly laziness' and 'the tyranny of unexamined assumptions'.[7] Perhaps the most damning comment is Robinson's perception of their 'almost wilful blindness' and of 'the consistent evasion by modern commentators of a solution they have already prejudged to be impossible'.[8]

Unfortunately, that summarizes much of contemporary biblical criticism for both the Old and the New Testament.

---

2 The precise origin of these lines is uncertain, but a helpful article can be found in 'The Love of God (1)', TanBible, http://www.tanbible.com/tol_sng/sng_theloveofgod.htm.
3 John A. T. Robinson, *Redating the New Testament* (London: SCM, 1976).
4 Ibid., p. 1.
5 Ibid., p. 229.
6 Ibid., p. 9.
7 Ibid., pp. 341, 345.
8 Ibid., p. 342.

1. Authentic Jesus

It might seem unnecessary to reconsider the evidence for the Jesus of history, but there are still a few who are determined to portray the Jesus revealed in Scripture as little more than a mythical figure invented by early Christian tradition.[9]

The evidence outside the Bible for the historical Jesus is well known and well documented. A brief survey is all that is required here.

Publius Cornelius Tacitus (AD 56–118) was a Roman senator and historian. His major work was entitled *Annals* and included the biography of Emperor Nero. In AD 64 the centre of Rome was engulfed in a horrific fire for which Nero was widely blamed. To turn attention from himself he harnessed a popular hatred of Christians, which resulted in terrible cruelty towards large numbers of them. We cannot help but wonder how many of those included in Paul's greetings in Romans 16 suffered at this time under Nero. Tacitus commented on this persecution and included the following:

Therefore, to put down the rumour, Nero substituted as culprits and punished in the most unusual ways those hated for their shameful acts ... Whom the crowd called Chrestians [sic]. The founder of this name, Christus, had been executed in the reign of Tiberius by the procurator Pontius Pilate ...[10]

Tacitus is regarded as a careful and accurate writer and the most reliable of all Roman historians. During his time as proconsul in Asia he would undoubtedly have gained an insight into the history of this 'foreign superstition', as Christianity was known. There is absolutely no scholarly reason to doubt his assertion of Christ's execution during the time of Emperor Tiberius by Pontius Pilate.

Flavius Josephus (AD 37–100) was a Jew born only four years after the crucifixion of Jesus; this makes him a credible witness to the history of the

---

9 See, for example, a recent symposium supporting this radical view: Thomas L. Thompson and Thomas S. Verenna (eds), *'Is This Not The Carpenter?' The Question of the Historicity of the Figure of Jesus* (New York: Routledge, 2014).
10 Tacitus, *Annals* XV.44.

times. Early in the Jewish revolt he was captured by the Romans but was eventually freed and lived in Rome more as a Roman than as a Jew. When Titus became emperor Josephus lived under the protection of Rome. His two great works, the *Jewish War* and *Jewish Antiquities*, defended the value of Judaism.

While Josephus remained an Orthodox Jew strongly committed to the values of Judaism, he nevertheless also often wrote more as a Roman than as a Jew and was never afraid to record what might have been unpopular among first-century Jews. In his *Jewish Antiquities* there are two clear references to Jesus. The first is his way of introducing James, who, he claims, was stoned to death on the orders of the high priest Ananus in AD 62. Josephus records that Ananus

assembled the sanhedrin of judges, and brought before them the brother of Jesus, who was called Christ [Messiah], whose name was James, and some others; and when he had formed an accusation against them as breakers of the law, he delivered them to be stoned.[11]

This martyrdom of James, the brother of Jesus and author of the New Testament letter, is not recorded in the Bible. Because James was a common Jewish name at this time, Josephus felt it necessary to identify him. The normal way would be to give the name of the father; however, Josephus must have recognized the significance of identifying James as the brother of Jesus 'who is called Christ'. Josephus is not endorsing that title but simply recording it. Historians have found no reason to doubt the genuineness of this text, nor, therefore, the reality of Jesus who was called the Messiah having a brother known as James who was stoned to death under the high priesthood of Ananus.

Another reference in *Jewish Antiquities* is disputed by many historians but should be mentioned:

Around this time there lived Jesus, a wise man, if indeed one ought to call him a man. For he was one who did surprising deeds, and a teacher of such people as accept the truth gladly. He won over many Jews and many of the Greeks. He was the Messiah.

---

11 *Antiquities* 20.9.1.

When Pilate, upon hearing him accused by men of the highest standing among us, had condemned him to be crucified, those who in the first place came to love him did not give up their affection for him, for on the third day, he appeared to them restored to life. The prophets of God had prophesied this and countless other marvellous things about him. And the tribe of Christians, so-called after him, has still to this day not died out. [12]

All existing manuscripts of the *Antiquities* contain this passage. However, it is generally assumed by historians that it was inserted by a later Christian editor, because it is considered unthinkable that Josephus, a Jew who strongly defended Judaism, would ever claim that Jesus was the Messiah or confirm his resurrection.

Significantly, the earliest existing Latin version says only that Jesus 'was believed to be the Messiah'; the Syriac version states, 'He was thought to be the Messiah'; and an Arabic version claims, 'He was perhaps the Messiah.' This may imply that a later Christian editor had made the claim more affirmative: 'He was the Messiah.' Whatever editorial changes there may have been, it is almost certain that the passage began life from the hand of Josephus, and there is no reason to doubt the confirmation that it was Pilate who ordered Jesus' crucifixion.

From these two authorities—Tacitus and Josephus—alone, any unprejudiced historian will conclude that there was a Jesus who had a brother named James, that he was known by some as the Messiah, he was accused by the Jewish authorities, condemned to be crucified on the orders of Pontius Pilate, governor of Judaea during the reign of Tiberius sometime between AD 26 and 36, and that his life and death gave rise to the new religion of Christians.

A foremost scholar on this subject records that, while it would have been in the interests of the early Jewish literature to demonstrate that Jesus was a mythical figure of Christianity, 'All Jewish sources treated Jesus as a fully historical person'; they simply reinterpreted the events of his life. [13]

---

12 Josephus, *Antiquities* 18.3.2.
13 Robert van Voorst, *Jesus Outside the New Testament: An Introduction to the Ancient Evidence* (Grand Rapids: Eerdmans, 2000). The following article may also prove helpful: 'The Historicity of Jesus Christ: Did He Really Exist?', The Divine Evidence, http://thedevineevidence.com/jesus_history.html.

Celsus was a Roman philosopher violently opposed to the Christian faith. Around the year AD 178 he published *True Discourse* as a vigorous argument against Christianity. Significantly, he never once argued against the true historicity of Jesus but simply reinterpreted all the events of his life. Here is part of his conclusion regarding the miracles of Jesus:

Jesus, on account of his poverty, was hired out to go to Egypt. While there he acquired certain [magical] powers ... It was by means of sorcery that he was able to accomplish the wonders which he performed ... Let us believe that these cures, or the resurrection, or the feeding of a multitude with a few loaves ... these are nothing more than the tricks of jugglers ...

On the virgin birth of Christ, Celsus concludes,

Jesus had come from a village in Judaea, and was the son of a poor Jewess who gained her living by the work of her hands. His mother had been turned out by her husband, who was a carpenter by trade, on being convicted of adultery [with a Roman soldier named Panthera]. Being thus driven away by her husband, and wandering about in disgrace, she gave birth to Jesus, a bastard.

There is much more in this vein about Jesus' life, the calling and sending out of the apostles, and then finally his crucifixion: 'Jesus accordingly exhibited after his death only the appearance of wounds received on the cross, and was not in reality so wounded as he is described to have been.'

No one disputes as other than genuine the tirade against Christianity by Celsus contained in *True Discourse*. Why did Celsus trouble to rubbish Christian belief in the life of Christ if the easier response would be simply to demonstrate that he never lived? In *Contra Celsum*, Origen, the church leader and theologian, wrote extensively against these views of Celsus.[14]

---

14 The work of Celsus is known almost entirely from the attack on it by Origen of Alexandria (180–253) in *Contra Celsum* (*Against Celsus*) written around AD 248. Historians do not doubt the accuracy of Origen's quotations from Celsus.

Lucian of Samosata (*c.* 120–180) was a second-century Greek satirist who ridiculed the Christians and Christ:

The Christians, you know, worship a man to this day. The distinguished person who introduced their novel rites, and was crucified on that account … It was impressed on them by their original lawgiver that they are all brothers from the moment they are converted and deny the gods of Greece, and worship the crucified sage, and live after his laws … [15]

Less directly confirming the historicity of Christ is the often-recorded evidence of Pliny the Younger when he was Roman governor of Bithynia-Pontus (now in modern Turkey). He wrote a letter to Emperor Trajan around AD 112 asking for advice on how to handle Christians in his area of control. Similarly, Suetonius, a Roman lawyer and historian between AD 69 and 122, wrote of the riots in Rome (AD 49) 'about Chrestus'. Bar-Serapion, a Stoic philosopher from Syria sometime after AD 70 (though some date his work as late as 200), wrote, 'What advantage did the Jews gain from executing their wise king? It was just after that their kingdom was abolished' [16]—a reference to the destruction of Jerusalem in AD 70.

It has to be acknowledged that there is not a single text in Jewish or pagan literature from the first few centuries that ever denies the historical reality of Jesus. In addition, we should remember that the disciples of Christ gave their lives for a belief in the life, death and resurrection of Jesus Christ, and the earliest church leaders, who would have known some of the apostles—Clement of Rome, Ignatius of Antioch, Polycarp of Smyrna, Papias of Phrygia—in all their writings never doubted the historical Jesus.

The suggestion that Jesus never existed is a purely modern idea without a speck of evidence. It is the gasp of timid critics who are unable to confront the massive challenge of who Jesus was, what he claimed, and all that he accomplished.

---

15 *The Death of Peregrinus*, 11–13.
16 See Robert E. Van Voors, *Jesus Outside the New Testament: An Introduction to the Ancient Evidence* (Grand Rapids: Eerdmans, 2000), pp. 53–55.

2. Authentic records

The common assumption has been that no one would have written of the events of the life of Christ or his teaching much before the close of the first century at the earliest; they circulated for around one hundred years as oral teaching, and during this time many myths and legends crept into the basic historical core.

This superficial assumption that the Gospels were not written down until long after the events is due partly to an ignorance of the widespread use of writing in the first century. One critic extravagantly claims, 'It is incontrovertible that in the earliest period there was only an oral record of the narrative and sayings of Jesus.'[17] The conclusion is that the Gospels are not history as we know it.

On the contrary, there was nothing unusual during the first century, and earlier, in a whole speech being accurately remembered and recorded. The art of memorizing was well advanced in an age that had little means of storing information. Even an oral passing-on of information would be presumed to be accurate. And more people could read than is generally imagined.

The text above the cross read 'JESUS OF NAZARETH, THE KING OF THE JEWS ... and the sign was written in Aramaic, Latin and Greek' (John 19:19–20). Clearly Pilate wanted everyone to read it, so it was in Aramaic and Greek; and he intended to get the message across to those who were in charge, so it was in Latin, the language of the occupying power.

There is nothing unusual about this. All over Palestine first-century texts have turned up in Aramaean, Nabatean, Greek, Hebrew and Latin, including marriage and divorce documents, food lists, orders for merchandise, soldiers' pay slips, legal documents and even graffiti. Not infrequently texts were in more than one language. When Mount Vesuvius erupted and engulfed Pompeii in AD 79 its legacy was to preserve

---

17 W. G. Kümmel, trans., *Introduction to the New Testament* (London: SCM, 1975), p. 55; quoted in Alan Millard, *Reading and Writing in the Time of Jesus* (Sheffield: Sheffield Academic Press, 2000), p. 8. Millard has presented a very strong case in favour of the written records. This section is indebted to him.

a snapshot of first-century Greek and Roman life. Writing appears everywhere, and thousands of inscriptions—political, advertising, love notes and the erotic—have been found scratched onto the walls. A local baker ensured that everyone would be impressed with his education by displaying a beautiful picture of himself and his wife holding a scroll and writing tablet.

The early Jewish Christians were schooled in the belief that the written word was final and authoritative, hence the high respect for the scrolls of the Torah. Although the Jewish rabbis and Greek and Roman philosophers preferred oral teaching, it is known that students of rabbis and philosophers kept notes of the instruction they received.

BOOKS AND NOTEBOOKS

Books were widely read in the first century: histories (Pliny and Josephus), agricultural practice (Columella), verse (Gallus and Virgil), satire (Petronius), philosophy (Seneca) and biography (Suetonius and Tacitus). There was a high degree of literacy at this time, and most people could read even if they could not write. More people owned books (or scrolls) than was once thought. The Ethiopian was reading his personal copy of the prophet Isaiah when Philip met him (Acts 8:28).

Every Jewish male was expected to be able to read, and no one would have been surprised when Zechariah requested a 'writing tablet' (Luke 1:63). It was common for civil servants and others to use 'notebooks' for their work; Matthew, Zacchaeus, the centurion, and the estate workers in the parable of Luke 16:6 were each able to read and write. Notebooks were an early form of book made of parchment sheets or thin layers of wood fastened together with rings. The Greek language borrowed the Latin name for this, which is *membranae*. This is exactly the word used in 2 Timothy 4:13 ('parchments'). Paul was using 'notebooks'.

A leading Jewish authority on the rabbis of this time concludes, '… we would naturally expect the logia [teaching] of Jesus to be originally copied in codices [books].'[18]

---

18 S. Lieberman, quoted in Millard, *Reading and Writing in the Time of Jesus*, p. 211.

We may be hesitant to suggest that the Gospels were written 'on the hoof', as the disciples accompanied Jesus, but it would be natural to expect some listeners to have written down his teaching and parables. This would be fully in keeping with what we know of the literacy and note-taking of first-century Palestine. There is no reason why the Gospel writers did not have access to written records made at the time—even their own.

The apostle Peter has shown himself, in his two short letters, to have been a master of good Greek. Inevitably, critics against Peter's authorship, especially of 2 Peter, have argued that a Galilean fisherman whose native language was Aramaic could hardly have been fluent in Greek. These critics appear to have forgotten that one of our greatest literary giants of the seventeenth century was John Bunyan, a mender of pots by trade; and that William Carey, who travelled to India in 1793, learned many Indian languages and dialects, and became professor of languages at Fort William College, was a cobbler before he left England; and that John Newton, the converted eighteenth-century slave trader, mastered Greek and Hebrew in order to read his Bible fluently and could correspond with Dutch theologians in Latin, yet his only formal education was two years at an inferior school in Essex. Benjamin Franklin, the American author, politician, diplomat, publisher, scientist and inventor, had no more than two years' formal education. Why then should not Peter the fisherman be capable of writing to the churches in excellent Greek?

MEMORIZING

We do well to remember that the art of memorizing has been largely lost in the world today. In the ancient world it was essential. The Greek historian Xenophon (c.430–354 BC) tells of an educated Greek called Nicolaus who could repeat by heart the whole of Homer's *Iliad* and *Odyssey*—all 24,000 lines! At the time of the English Reformation John Mandrel could neither read nor write, but he obtained a copy of Tyndale's Bible and carried it around with him; whenever he met someone who could read, he asked that person to read him passages from the Bible, and in this way he learned large parts of the Scriptures by heart. Closer to our time, Alexander Solzhenitsyn, while in a Soviet labour camp, wrote passages on scraps of paper, memorized them, destroyed the evidence, and on release could commit to writing 12,000 lines from memory. Similarly, the Romanian pastor Richard Wurmbrand, who was sent to a Soviet gulag in 1948 and confined to an underground cell for three years, kept his mind alert by preaching a sermon to himself every night. By fixing them with mnemonics and rhymes, on his release he recorded over three hundred sermons.

Why then is it 'incontrovertible that in the earliest period there was only an oral record of the narrative and sayings of Jesus'? And why should we doubt the accuracy of the ancient memory, particularly in sermons so important from the lips of Christ? And on what historical grounds can we doubt the written records of his teaching from the very earliest days?

Critical wishful thinking may be whistling in the dark, but it is not evidence.

3. Authentic narratives

There are many episodes in the Gospels that bear all the marks of eyewitness accounts.

John is careful to reveal himself as both the writer of the Gospel that bears his name and an eyewitness to the events. At the close of John's Gospel he introduces the account of Peter's declaration of love to the risen Christ as the disciples breakfasted by the Sea of Galilee; that interview closes with Peter referring to John himself. Although John does not give his name but only talks of 'the disciple whom Jesus loved' and who had been beside Christ at the Last Supper, it is agreed that this can refer only to John. He then concludes, 'This is the disciple who testifies to these things and who wrote them down. We know that his testimony is true' (John 21:24). At the beginning of his first short letter, John underscores the fact that he was a personal witness to all that Christ did and taught during his three years of public ministry (1 John 1:1–3).

Before such claims are dismissed as forgeries, remember the correct legal requirement: 'The character of the author of a document is to be considered trustworthy unless or until it is proven otherwise. A witness is presumed credible until the contrary is shown.' Those who dismiss these eyewitness accounts must bring forward their evidence, not their wishful thinking. We are here presenting the evidence in favour of their claims and we are entitled to allow the characters of New Testament writers to speak for themselves.

The evidence of eyewitnesses is frequently referred to in the Gospels. At the crucifixion, 'all those who knew him, including the women who had followed him from Galilee, stood at a distance, watching these things' (Luke 23:49). The references to Joseph and Nicodemus as members of the Jewish parliament (Luke 23:50; John 3:1; 19:39) would be dangerous insertions if no such men ever existed. Even decades after the event, such claims could easily be checked in the Jewish records.

The vivid detail of Mark's Gospel is frequently acknowledged as evidence of authentic writing. Over forty times Mark employs the word *euthus* ('immediately') to express the movement from one event to the next, and his detail of the 'green grass' (6:39) is not one that any ancient writer would invent simply to make his narrative appear authentic; the earliest forgers were not that smart.

For his part, Luke does not claim personally to have been an eyewitness to everything he records, but his emphasis is upon the painstaking care with which he sourced his material. Luke recognized that many had already written accounts of the life and ministry of Christ, which is only what we would expect. It is inconceivable that, in a literate age when people were busy writing and reading books, the new disciples of Christ would have been content simply to pass on oral gossip—for which we have no evidence at all.

Luke specifically informs us that many had 'undertaken to draw up an account' from eyewitnesses who were with Christ from the very first (Luke 1:1). Luke's commitment to careful research and an orderly description so that Theophilus might be reassured of the certainty of what he had already been told must either be taken at face value and trusted, or else we are dealing with a cheat and liar of the first order for which evidence must be produced (Luke 1:1–4).

Anyone who reads the four Gospels and the writing of the apostles must acknowledge the unique life of Christ and the pure morality that he taught and that his disciples expounded in their letters. To dismiss them all as blatant liars and forgers demands a massive leap of unbelieving faith!

It is the responsibility of the critic to show wherever or whenever they reneged on their faith in Christ or the moral standards they upheld. Most of them died for their passionate belief in the perfect life and literal resurrection of Christ.

PHILIP'S INTRODUCTION OF JESUS TO NATHANAEL

John's Gospel relates how Philip introduced Nathanael to Jesus. It is a simple narrative, but the dialogue is significant:

Philip found Nathanael and told him, 'We have found the one Moses wrote about in the Law, and about whom the prophets also wrote—Jesus of Nazareth, the son of Joseph.' 'Nazareth! Can anything good come from there?' Nathanael asked (John 1:45–46).

If this episode had been invented by a writer sometime in the second century, why would he refer to 'Jesus of Nazareth', when everyone by then knew that Jesus had been born in Bethlehem, which was the town foretold by the prophet Micah (5:2)? Nazareth is nowhere mentioned in the Old Testament, nor did it form any part of the Jewish expectations of the Messiah. And why would this writer refer to him as 'the son of Joseph', when long before the second century Jesus was widely referred to as 'the Son of God' or at least 'the son of Mary'?

There is only one explanation for all this: it is a precise record of the conversation between Philip and Nathanael.

JESUS WRITING ON THE GROUND

In John 8 we have the account of the woman taken in the act of adultery and brought before Jesus for his verdict on her. This passage is often disputed because it does not appear in some of the earliest manuscripts. Leaving aside the discussion of textual criticism, one argument for its authenticity is found in that strange and unexplained action of Jesus'. Faced with the insistent questioning by the Jews, the Gospel records, 'Jesus bent down and started to write on the ground with his finger' (v. 6).

What did he write? We have no idea. So why did the writer of the Gospel bother to 'invent' such an irrelevant piece of meaningless information? C. S. Lewis was a recognized scholar of English literature and he responded to this Gospel episode thus: 'As a literary historian, I am perfectly convinced that whatever else the Gospels are, they are not legends. I have read a great deal of legend and I am quite clear they are not the same sort of thing … The art of inventing little irrelevant details to make an imaginary scene more convincing is a purely modern art.' Lewis maintained that this episode is a mark of authentic writing; it is what actually happened and was recorded by an eyewitness.[19]

JOHN'S RELATIONSHIP TO THE HIGH PRIEST

There are many more of these authentic details. Here is another that is often overlooked: 'Simon Peter and another disciple were following Jesus. Because this disciple was known to the high priest, he went with Jesus into the high priest's courtyard, but Peter had to wait outside at the door. The other disciple, who was known to the high priest, came back, spoke to the girl on duty there and brought Peter in' (John 18:15–16).

We may well ask how John, a Galilean fisherman (who here refers to himself as 'the other disciple), would have been known to the high priest. We are not told what John's relationship with the high priest was that enabled him to gain access to the courtyard—but why invent it? The story of Peter's denial does not need this insert. Had the Gospel writer simply told us that Peter and John entered the courtyard, we would have asked no more questions; after all, why should they not? At this distance of time we do not know the protocol for gaining access to the courtyard. The insertion of this seemingly irrelevant fact raises questions and answers none. It is another mark of an authentic record.

---

19 C. S. Lewis, 'What Are We to Make of Jesus Christ?', Essay, 1950; in Lyle W. Dorsett, (ed.), *The Essential C. S. Lewis* (Nashville: B&H, 1999).

THE DEATH, BURIAL AND RESURRECTION OF JESUS

If later writers were wanting their readers to believe that Jesus is the Son of God and Lord of creation, the account of his journey to Golgotha was a disaster. Apparently he was too weak to carry the crossbeam (Matt. 27:32). And who would make up the cry from the cross: 'My God, my God, why have you forsaken me?' (27:46). Unless Christ really died in the manner recorded in the Gospels, only a fool would try to turn a weak and broken gibbeted criminal into a resurrected hero and Saviour.

Everything about the tomb fits all that we know of the burial of wealthy people at that time. In a new tomb the body would be close to the entrance and therefore easily visible (John 20:5); the rolled stone was used only for the tombs of the rich (Matt. 27:57, 60). And notice the detail recorded in John 20:7–8: 'the burial cloth that had been around Jesus' head … was folded up by itself, separate from the linen.' Again, that has the hallmark of an eyewitness detail.

The various accounts of the resurrection have often been accused of confusion and contradiction. In reality it is possible to demonstrate how they all connect.[20] We do not have to be certain that a reconstruction of the events of those emotionally charged hours after the disappearance of the body is necessarily correct in every detail; we have only to show that it is a reasonable reconstruction of what might well have taken place.

THE PROMISED RETURN OF CHRIST

If the Gospels were compiled in the second century or any time after the lives of the apostles, why did the editors include the puzzling verses in Matthew 24 that imply the return of Christ in 'this generation', when it was evident to all that he had not returned 'with power and great glory' (vv. 30–34)? Commentators have debated this for centuries, but any writer inventing the teaching of Jesus long after his death would have been a fool to invent a promise that apparently had not been fulfilled as predicted.

---

20 See, for example, Clive Anderson and Brian Edwards, *Evidence for the Bible* (Leominster: Day One, 2014), pp. 218–210.

THE ANCESTRY OF THE MESSIAH

If a pious Christian was inventing the line of Israel's Messiah, consider the unlikely ancestry recorded in Matthew 1. Why start with Judah (vv. 2–3)? He was hardly the best of the twelve sons of Isaac. He sold his youngest brother into slavery, lied to his father, deceived a neighbouring tribe and slaughtered them, failed to keep his promises, and consorted with someone he thought was a prostitute but who was in reality his daughter-in-law, Tamar. Hardly a bright light in the Messiah's ancestry. Joseph would have been a better choice: he was the favourite son from the favourite wife, and his is a big story of a quality life—an excellent example to follow. And why include Rahab, who was a Canaanite and prostitute, and Ruth, who was a Moabite (v. 5)? Both came from a people who were enemies of Israel. And for what purpose is there the indirect reference to David's tragic double sin of adultery and murder (v. 6)? Surely a Christian inventing the genealogy would keep the line pure and confined to Israel, and the moral failure of David would best be forgotten? All this is a mark of an authentic genealogy.

JAIRUS'S DAUGHTER

On a number of occasions Jesus ordered a healed person not to tell everyone what had happened, but nowhere is this more unusual than in Mark 5:43. When Jesus arrived at the home of Jairus, the synagogue ruler, there was already a 'commotion, with people crying and wailing loudly'—Matthew calls it a 'noisy crowd' (Matt. 9:23). Jesus took his disciples and the parents of the girl into her room and raised her from death. When she appeared to the mourners it would have been obvious that a miracle had been accomplished, so why did Jesus 'give strict orders not to let anyone know about this'? Luke agrees with this statement (Luke 8:56).

This has intrigued commentators for centuries, and the seeming absurdity of it could not have escaped the Gospel writers Mark and Luke. So why did they insert that strange command? Because, for whatever reason, that is what Jesus said. Perhaps it was Jesus' way of making it clear that he was not performing miracles in order to spread his fame but because of his compassion. However, spread his fame this miracle most certainly did, as Matthew records (Matt. 9:26).

THE BLIND MAN AT BETHSAIDA

The account in Mark 8:22–26 is unusual for a number of reasons. Mark is well known for his detail, and here are some unusual features unlike those in the other healing miracles of Jesus. Why do we need to know that Jesus 'took the blind man by the hand and led him outside the village'? Commentators and preachers will doubtless find an explanation—perhaps the man did not live in the village and was brought there to beg every day, so Jesus was saying, 'You will soon not need to beg any more' (see v. 26)—but it is a detail that would hardly be invented. And why did Jesus spit on the man's eyes? That is something that is never recorded of any of his other miracles. And why was this man uniquely healed in two stages? There is no certain answer to any of these questions except that, as with John's account of Jesus writing on the ground with his finger, it just happened that way, so Mark recorded it.

WASHING THE DISCIPLES' FEET

John 13 records the occasion when Jesus, during the Last Supper, took a towel and washed his disciples' feet. Not only was this a most unlikely thing for Jesus to have done unless it actually happened, but also the details of the account are graphically described. Each action was burnt into John's mind. The small word 'so' in verse 4 is significant. In the light of the three things just previously stated—that the Father had put all things under his power, and that Jesus Christ had come from God and was returning to God—therefore ('so') he humbled himself to wash his disciples' feet. The contrast could not have been greater between who Christ claimed to be and what he now did. John seems determined to present the absurdity of it all by describing graphically what happened. It is an act hard to imagine John inventing in the light of his exalted view of Jesus, who he has presented from the very first chapter of his Gospel as the Creator and perfect expression of God.

WHAT YOUNG MAN?

At the arrest of Jesus, Mark introduces us to an unnamed young man who slipped out of his linen garment and fled naked into the night when the thugs tried to seize him (Mark 14:51–52). Who was this young man and why is it important? Among many suggested identifications, the most likely is that this was John Mark himself, the writer of this Gospel, and it was his coded way of showing that he was an eyewitness to these dramatic events. If so, why did he not refer to himself directly and remove all doubt? 'I was there' would have been impressive. But if this was not John Mark, why did he insert the episode at all? It is hardly relevant for anything. Either way, it is a mark of an authentic record. If it is a code for Mark himself, then we have evidence of the Gospel writer as an eyewitness to these events; and if it is not a reference to himself, then it is yet another irrelevant detail that only an eyewitness would insert.

PAUL'S HAIRCUT!

Even Luke, the meticulous historian, introduces his share of seemingly irrelevant details. Acts 18 records Paul in Corinth in Greece and travelling from there to Syria. However, at the port of Cenchrea 'he had his hair cut off … because of a vow' (v. 18). Apart from it being the home town of Phoebe (Rom. 16:1), this is the only reference to Cenchrea in the New Testament. Why Paul would have done this, and what the vow was all about, Luke does not tell us. So why did he bother to refer to it? Clearly it was significant at the time and therefore Luke included it in his journal. For the reasons C. S. Lewis gave on John 8 (see page 27), this is not the sort of detail that would be invented by an ancient narrative forger.

4. Authentic 'contradictions'

Many of the narratives from the ministry of Christ are repeated across the four Gospels, and in some cases there are discrepancies in the accounts which are inevitably assumed by the critics to be contradictions. This is not the place to resolve in detail these assumed contradictions; that has been done by scores of commentaries on the Gospels.[21] One example here will suffice.

---

21 The subject of supposed errors and contradictions is dealt with in more detail in Brian Edwards, *Nothing But the Truth* (Darlington: Evangelical Press, 3rd edn. 2006), pp. 415–465.

BLIND BARTIMAEUS

Matthew 20:30 mentions two blind men at Jericho, while Mark and Luke refer to only one (Mark 10:46; Luke 18:35). Luke also states that the episode took place as Jesus 'approached' Jericho, while Matthew and Mark claim he was 'leaving' Jericho.

Mark and Luke do not deny there were two men; they simply concern themselves with only one, Bartimaeus, perhaps because they focus on the one who was, or became, the better known of the two; this is implied by Mark's reference to the father of Bartimaeus (Mark 10:46). It is common for news commentators today to focus on the more notorious of those involved in an incident. Similarly, in another narrative, Matthew refers to two demoniacs while Mark and Luke mention only one (Matt. 8:28; Mark 5:2; Luke 8:26–27).

In the account of the blind men, did Christ heal as they entered or as they left Jericho? The simplest explanation is to reconstruct the episode like this: the blind men were sitting at the entrance of the city and began calling to Jesus as he passed by. He took no notice and the crowd ordered them to be silent. His refusal to stop and listen at once was not unusual in Jesus' ministry when he wanted to draw out a stronger appeal to himself; it is similar to what we read in the account of the Canaanite woman in Matthew 15:21–28. Jesus entered the city, met Zacchaeus and probably stayed at his home overnight. During the evening or early morning, the blind men crossed the city to renew their appeal as Jesus left in the morning. It was on this occasion that Jesus stopped and healed them.

This reconstruction assumes that the Gospel writers decided not to break up the story before and after our Lord's night in Jericho but to complete it as one event. Matthew and Mark recorded it on the departure because that is when the appeal was answered, and Luke dealt with it on the entry, because that is when the appeal began. If we take Luke 19:1, 'Jesus entered Jericho and was passing through', as a reference to the story of Bartimaeus and not to the story of Zacchaeus, then we have Luke's way of telling us that the events he has just related actually took place as Christ came into and came out of the city—in perfect harmony with Matthew and Mark's accounts.

We do not have to prove that this is a correct reconstruction, only that it is reasonable and therefore quite possible. There would only be a contradiction if we knew everything that could be known about the episode and still we could not harmonize the differences. If we are told that a friend has been killed in a terrible accident on a motorway, and we subsequently discover that he died in hospital of his injuries three days later, it would never occur to us that our first informant was either misinformed or misleading us.

THE SERMONS OF JESUS

If we compare the sermons of Jesus in the Gospels we will discover differences between one account and another. However, like any preacher of good news, Jesus almost certainly dealt with the same subject—even illustrating with the same parables—on more than one occasion and with variations. Even when the Gospel writers record the same sermon on the same occasion, we must never assume that what we have in our Bible is necessarily the full text of all that Jesus said. If he spent the whole day teaching, there would have been a deal of repetition as the crowds came and went, just as any open-air preacher knows. Assuming his almost daily teaching over the three years of his public ministry, we have only about one thousandth part of all that Jesus said.

Critics cannot have it both ways: these discrepancies are clear evidence that the Gospel writers were compiling their work independently of each other, and that makes the wide degree of agreement in detail even more impressive. If they were all working from the same source they would not knowingly introduce differences. On the other hand, if the writers were always identical when recording the same event, we can be sure that some would assume they were all using a single source and that therefore we do not have four independent witnesses. Yet because there are apparent contradictions here and there, the accusation is that we cannot rely on their accounts. The fallacy and prejudice of all this are obvious.

SOURCE Q?

Incidentally, if any reader is aware of the endless discussions surrounding a possible mysterious source 'Q' that was supposedly a common source of material for Matthew, Mark and Luke, it may help to sideline this myth. There is no known source 'Q'; it is only a theory to explain the similarities within these three Gospels. Whether or not these three writers had access to some common material is quite unimportant. Q may exist more in the minds of scholars than in reality. We have already seen how writing and note-taking was commonplace in the first century, and there is no reason why a literate accountant like Matthew might not have kept his own notebook of sermons and events.

5. Authentic silence

THE CLOSURE OF ACTS

Scriptwriters and novelists spend hours ensuring they have the best 'closure' for their plays or novels, even for every instalment. Readers of the Acts of the Apostles will find its closure frustrating. The dramatic and exciting events of the life of Paul are brought to a sudden and unexpected end. Acts does not conclude; it simply stops! On trial for his life before Emperor Nero and with a stated desire to continue with his evangelism by visiting Spain, Paul is left for two years 'in his own rented house' in Rome, entertaining his friends and preaching (Acts 28:30–31). But what happened next? It is inconceivable that anyone making up this account in the late first or early second century would not have finished the story. Paul as a heroic martyr is exactly what the early churches would have expected and needed.

Of the many suggestions as to why the record closes so abruptly and tantalizingly, the most convincing is that this is as far as events had progressed when Luke wrote. If Luke did complete the account later we have no evidence of it. The record, finishing where it does, undermines any suggestion that it is an invented story; on the contrary, it provides evidence that the Gospel of Luke and its sequel in Acts were completed before the death of Paul. Both, therefore, are likely to have been completed before AD 64 or 67. To question this conclusion, strong facts must be forthcoming, not vague theories.

THE DESTRUCTION OF THE TEMPLE

As we noted at the start of Part 1 (see page 15), the silence of the New Testament regarding the destruction of the temple and city of Jerusalem is strong evidence for the completion of the New Testament, or at least most of it, before the year AD 70. That event would have served the purpose of many of the New Testament writers as a visual aid to prove that God had finished with the old covenant of ceremonies, priests, sacrifices and temple. This was a major theme of the letter to the Hebrews, for example, yet no word of that horrific destruction appears. Nor does it appear as a postscript in the Gospel records, where Jesus prophesied the destruction of the temple (Matt. 24:1–2; Mark 13:1–2; Luke 21:5–6). Nor is it even hinted at in the final book of the New Testament, where Christ and his gospel are presented as ultimately vindicated and victorious.

The most reasonable conclusion from this total silence on what Robinson called 'the most ... climactic event of the period' is that it had not taken place when the Gospels and Epistles of the New Testament were complete.

6. Authentic history

The missionary journeys of Paul and the letters that he wrote to the newly planted churches are mid-first century; of this there can be no serious doubt. Early church leaders were quoting from them by the turn of the first century, and to assume that the events recorded in the Acts of the Apostles were invented sometime in the second century is too extreme to be considered worthy of rebuttal. However 'primitive' the early churches may have been, they were certainly not that gullible. The Acts of the Apostles presupposes the reality of the life, death, resurrection and ascension of Jesus Christ. The fact that the Gospels and Acts are first-century documents is evidenced by the detail that has been confirmed by archaeology.

CAESAR'S CENSUS

The mention of the requirement of every man to return to his home for the purposes of taxation (Luke 2:2) was once challenged as an unnecessary upheaval that would never have been ordered; that was until a papyrus document was discovered early in the twentieth century and dated to the time of Emperor Trajan in AD 104, in which the Roman governor of Egypt ordered every man to return to his own 'hearth' (home) for the purpose of registration. Similarly, the claim that Pilate was governor of Judaea (Luke 3:1) was questioned by some until an inscription from Caesarea, discovered in 1961, confirmed the fact.

LUKE, PAUL'S TRAVEL COMPANION

From Acts 16:10 to 28:16, Luke, the author of the Acts of the Apostles, includes himself as a companion of Paul by using the pronouns 'we' and 'us' almost sixty times. The first reference is in Troas—although there is no reason why Luke might not have been with Paul even before then—and the last is in Rome. Luke might not have been an eyewitness to all the events he recorded in Acts, but clearly he was a close companion of Paul's, and the many hours of travel by land and sea provided adequate time to catch up on the details from Paul himself.[22]

In his Gospel and Acts Luke names 117 living people, 114 towns, provinces, islands, seas and other identifiable places, and 25 political, military, social or religious events known to history.

This amount of information implies that the author must have kept a journal. To avoid confusion, he often provides details to identify exactly who he means: such as Judas 'the Galilean'; Lydia, 'a trader in purple dye'; Simon 'the tanner'; Sceva, 'a chief priest'; Crispus, 'the synagogue ruler'; Simeon 'called Niger'; and Judas, who lived in Damascus 'on Straight Street'.

Luke's order of events, his location of towns and provinces, and his knowledge of Roman administration, censuses and regiments, and of Jewish rituals, law and festivals, are faultless. His reference to the famine across Judaea (Acts 11:28–29) fits precisely what we know of the devastating famine in AD 45 from the writings of both the Jewish historian Josephus (*Antiquities* 20.2.5) and the Roman historians Suetonius (*The Life of Claudius* 18) and Tacitus (*Annals* 11.4). Similarly, Luke refers

---

22 See Donald Guthrie, *New Testament Introduction*, vol. 3, *Gospels and Acts* (London: Tyndale Press, 1965), a masterful and conclusive defence of Luke as the author of the Gospel and Acts and the subject of the 'we' passages.

to the expulsion of the Jews from Rome by Claudius (Acts 18:2), an act confirmed by Suetonius (*The Life of Claudius* 25.4).[23] The death of Herod Agrippa recorded in Acts 12:21–23 fits perfectly with the description by the contemporary Jewish historian Josephus (*Antiquities* 19.8.2).

Luke's references to Gallio at Corinth (Acts 18:12), Sergius Paulus at Paphos (Acts 13:7) and Paul's reference to Erastus as the city's 'director of public works' (Rom. 16:23) are all confirmed by inscriptions.[24]

Luke's naming of national and local officials and the collective name of civic councils, which differed from town to town, match precisely what we know to be the case. One example of this is his reference to the town council at Thessalonica as *politarchas*—translated as 'city officials' (Acts 17:6). A second-century Roman arch discovered in Thessalonica in 1876 names some of the officials in the city and the first word is *poleitarchounton*, which means 'to act as a polytarch'. Four men listed on the inscription—Sosipatros, Lucius, Secundus and Gaius—are names found in the New Testament; they are not the same men, but they confirm a first-century context for Acts.

Elsewhere, Luke accurately describes Philippi as a Roman colony whose officials were *stratēgoi* ('magistrates', 16:38). In Ephesus the 'officials of the province' are called the *asiarchōn* (19:31), exactly the title of those whom we know controlled religious affairs. At Malta the *prōtos* ('chief official', 28:7) was in charge. All these titles are found on inscriptions of that time in the various towns. These are facts that would never have been known to later generations and are clear evidence that Luke was an eyewitness of all that he recorded.

The precision of Luke 3:1–2, which refers to the start of the ministry of John the Baptist, is a model of historical detail. There can be no doubt that Luke is relating an actual event and the year is precisely AD 29, since Tiberius came to power in AD 14.

In the fifteenth year of the reign of Tiberius Caesar—when Pontius Pilate was governor of Judaea, Herod tetrarch of Galilee, his brother Philip tetrarch of Iturea

---

23 Anderson and Edwards, *Evidence for the Bible*, pp. 154–155.
24 Ibid., pp. 156, 166–167.

and Traconitis, and Lysanias tetrarch of Abilene—during the high priesthood of Annas and Caiaphas, the word of God came to John son of Zechariah in the desert.

Similarly, the details of Paul's journey from Jerusalem to Rome (Acts 27–28) are without precedent in ancient records of travel. Luke's attention to detail in the narrative is fascinating. For example, in Acts 20:13 we read, 'We went on ahead to the ship and sailed for Assos, where we were going to take Paul aboard. He had made this arrangement because he was going there on foot.' Luke offers no reason for Paul's decision to walk the thirty-one miles on the Roman road from Troas to Assos rather than travel with his companions by sea. It is a clear mark of authentic history that a small fact is stated without explanation.

The precision of Acts 27:37—'Altogether there were 276 of us on board'—again reflects Luke's attention to detail.

After a lifetime of archaeological study in Asia Minor (modern-day Turkey), Sir William Mitchell Ramsay, one of the foremost New Testament scholars of the nineteenth and early twentieth centuries, concluded of Luke's record in Acts, 'It could bear the most minute scrutiny as an authority for the facts of the Aegean world, and it was written with such judgement, skill, art and perception of truth as to be a model of historical statement.' Ramsay went further: 'I set out to look for truth on the borderland where Greece and Asia meet, and found it there [in Acts]. You may press the words of Luke in a degree beyond any other historian's and they stand the keenest scrutiny and the hardest treatment.' The conclusion of this eminent New Testament scholar and historian was: 'Christianity did not originate in a lie, and we can and ought to demonstrate this, as well as to believe it.' [25]

THE CENTURIONS OF ACTS

At least five centurions are referred to in the New Testament; two are found in the Acts of the Apostles, and both are described as belonging to regular Roman regiments. Cornelius was 'a centurion in what was known as the

---

25 Ramsay, *The Bearing of Recent Discovery on the Trustworthiness of the New Testament*, pp. 85, 89.

Italian Regiment' (10:1), and Julius 'belonged to the Imperial [literally, 'the Augustan'] Regiment' (27:1). In spite of Luke's proven attention to accurate detail, some Roman historians assumed an error here on the basis that Rome employed only local Sebasteni (auxiliary) regiments in Palestine, and that a unit made up of Roman citizens would not have been placed under the command of a Jewish governor like Agrippa. However, this assumption has been shown to be in error. Tomb inscriptions of Roman soldiers clearly reveal that Roman citizens served with local auxiliaries. One leading authority states that 'Roman troops stationed in client states, side by side with native irregulars, are not unusual'. He further adds that Luke's reference to Julius reveals a 'factual accuracy in a point where it had been doubted the most ... With the help of inscriptions the Acts are further shown to report with great reliability the name, the officer and the escort duties of the Augustan cohort.'[26]

The same authority comments that Luke's narrative of Paul's arrest in Jerusalem, his trial at Caesarea, and his journey by sea to Rome 'is an eyewitness account that has the compelling ring of historical truth. Its detailed observations are a first-class source for ancient sea travel and shipwreck and no less for the police duties of the Roman army.'[27]

7. Authentic honesty

In the four Gospels there is an embarrassing honesty in the unbelief of the disciples with regard to who Jesus was and also in their frequent squabbling. Why would anyone invent the episode of the disciples arguing among themselves who would be the greatest in the kingdom of God (Luke 22:24)? Or the request of James and John for preferential treatment there (Mark 10:35–45)? It shows them all in the worst possible light.

And why invent the rebuke of Jesus to his disciples for their slowness to believe the Old Testament prophets (Luke 24:25)? In fact, throughout

---

26 A detailed and authoritative vindication of Luke's accuracy on this point is found in M. P. Speidel, 'The Roman Army in Judaea under the Procurators', *Ancient Society* 13/14 (1982/83), pp. 231–240.

27 Ibid.

their three years with Jesus, they were incapable of grasping the full reality of who he was and what he had come to do; they blunder into mistaken conclusions and betray their lack of faith on many occasions. There is not a hero among them. We can almost hear the note of exasperation in the response of Jesus shortly before his death: 'You believe at last!' (John 16:31). We despair at their unbelief and yet marvel at the honesty of the record. There is no rational explanation as to why second-century forgers would show the disciples of Christ in such a poor light; if they were seeking to authenticate the apostles as the pillars and foundation of the infant church, this would be a very strange way to do so.

It is noteworthy that, in the account of the death and resurrection of Jesus, it is the women who are the most believing and the first on the scene. They are present at the cross when few disciples were (Matt. 27:55–56; Mark 15:40–41; Luke 23:55; John 19:25), and they were the first at the tomb and the first to meet with the risen Christ (Matt. 28:1–9; Mark 16:1–11; Luke 24:1–8; John 20:1, 10–18).

Would later writers have invented these crucial roles for women in an age of male pre-eminence? It was a terrible put-down to the masculine pride of the first and second centuries—and beyond! Surely it was the inner band of disciples who should have been the first to witness the resurrection? The only reason the women are centre stage is because that is precisely where they were. In fact, the men at first dismissed their account as lunacy (Luke 24:10–11).

8. Authentic letters

No one can read the New Testament letters with an unbiased mind without the conviction that this is real correspondence from real men to real churches composed of real people with real issues at a real time in history.

In spite of this—and despite the fact that the earliest list of New Testament books, the Muratorian Canon, dated around AD 150, includes all thirteen letters of Paul, and that few questioned the authorship of Paul until the nineteenth-century critics got to work—there are still some who insist that Paul wrote at the most half of the letters that bear his name.

Their reasons are unconvincing and have been shown to be so by able New Testament scholars.[28] We must never forget the challenge that these accounts have the right to be accepted as authentic unless and until they are proved false beyond reasonable doubt.

PERSONAL GREETINGS

The New Testament letters are full of personal references. In all the known 'pseudepigrapha' (false writing claiming to come from an apostle) of the first two or three centuries, there is nothing like this. Literature of this period never invented lists of imaginary people simply to make the work appear authentic. The closing greetings of Paul's letter to the church at Rome are sent to twenty-six people by name; almost half are women, and all of them are given specific greetings. The personal details are either the work of a master forger and supreme liar or they are evidence of an authentic letter dictated by Paul and written down by Tertius (Rom. 16:22).

Greet Priscilla and Aquila, my fellow-workers in Christ Jesus. They risked their lives for me. Not only I but all the churches of the Gentiles are grateful to them. Greet also the church that meets at their house. Greet my dear friend Epenetus, who was the first convert to Christ in the province of Asia. Greet Mary, who worked very hard for you. Greet Andronicus and Junias, my relatives who have been in prison with me. They are outstanding among the apostles, and they were in Christ before I was. Greet Ampliatus, whom I love in the Lord. Greet Urbanus, our fellow-worker in Christ, and my dear friend Stachys. Greet Apelles, tested and approved in Christ. Greet those who belong to the household of Aristobulus. Greet Herodion, my relative. Greet those in the household of Narcissus who are in the Lord. Greet Tryphena and Tryphosa, those women who work hard in the Lord. Greet my dear friend Persis, another woman who has worked very hard in the Lord. Greet Rufus, chosen in the Lord, and his mother, who has been a mother to me, too. Greet Asyncritus, Phlegon, Hermes, Patrobas, Hermas and the brothers with them. Greet Philologus, Julia, Nereus and his sister, and Olympas and all the saints with them (Rom. 16:3–15).

---

28 Perhaps the most scholarly and comprehensive is Guthrie, *New Testament Introduction*. It is still unsurpassed in its scholarly research and detail in defence of the authorship and authenticity of the New Testament.

In addition, Paul commends Phoebe to the church, and includes Timothy, Lucius, Jason, Sosipater, Tertius, Gaius, Erastus and Quartus, who each insisted on sending their greetings to the Christians at Rome. A total of thirty-five named people would never have been invented (and never were) by the false writings of a few decades later. Incidentally, Erastus is introduced by Paul as 'the city's director of public works' at Corinth, a claim that would be very easy to verify—and it has been: his name was discovered in 1929 outside the theatre at Corinth inscribed on a marble pavement that he had laid at his own expense.[29]

With one exception, each of Paul's letters contains the names of others, in the greeting either to begin or to close, or both. This format is a hallmark of Paul's letters. The one exception is Galatians, where there are no personal greetings at either end—although Paul does refer by name to Peter, James, John and Barnabas in connection with his conversion and subsequent visit to Jerusalem. The false writings attributed to Paul betray themselves by the fact that they never include these personal details.

As for the other apostles: in his two letters, Peter mentions only Silas, John Mark and Paul. James and Jude in their letters provide no names at all; they were writing to the churches generally rather than to specific congregations and it was not their style to add personal greetings. John mentions no one in his first letter, deliberately does not identify the church (or individual) he addresses in his second, and his third letter is sent to Gaius, with Diotrephes condemned and Demetrius warmly commended.

However, the authentic nature of the New Testament letters goes far beyond the greetings that top and tail many of them.

ISSUES AND PLANS

All the letters claiming to come from the hand of Paul are dealing with specific issues facing the churches. For example, the Galatians are being led astray by false teaching, the Colossians are in danger of being sidetracked by empty philosophy, the Corinthians are, among much else, weak in discipline and divided by factions, and the Ephesians need to learn the lesson of unity.

---

29 See Anderson and Edwards, *Evidence for the Bible*, p. 166.

Paul's comment about having to confront Peter, whose commitment to the gospel of faith alone for salvation had slipped, and the fact that 'even Barnabas' had been led astray (Gal. 2:11–13), would never have been invented by a later writer when Peter was held in such high esteem; it is evidence of an authentic letter from Paul written at a time of a theological crossroads for the infant church.

The cross-references to earlier letters are also hallmarks of authentic writing. When Paul dealt firmly with the Corinthian tolerance of an immoral member (1 Cor. 5), his strident commands were eventually heeded. Later, the man who had been disciplined came to repentance and the church was then at a loss to know how to deal with him. Paul wrote again (2 Cor. 2), encouraging them to a pastoral restoration of the repentant man.

Similarly, Paul continued his correspondence with the Thessalonians, clearing up in 2 Thessalonians 2:1, 5 some misunderstandings that had arisen from his first letter. His references to his previous visits or letters sent (2 Cor. 1:15; 2:1; 7:8; 13:1; 1 Thes. 2:1; 2 Thes. 2:5) are all evidence of authentic writing.

Paul's projected plans are a further evidence of authentic writing. He hoped to call on the Christians at Rome on his way to Spain (Rom. 15:24), and to spend the winter with the Corinthians after he had visited their near neighbours in Macedonia; meanwhile he would remain in Ephesus until Pentecost (1 Cor. 16:5–8). Even in his second letter to them (it was possibly his third) he expresses his intention of returning to them (2 Cor. 13:2, 10).

COMINGS AND GOINGS

There are frequent references to fellow-workers coming and going among the churches. Phoebe will arrive in Rome (Rom. 16:1–2). Tychicus will be sent to Ephesus shortly (Eph. 6:21) and Timothy to Philippi (Phil. 2:19). Epaphroditus, so willingly spared by the Philippians to assist Paul, will be coming back soon to demonstrate that he is fully recovered from his near-fatal illness, over which the church has been so concerned (2:25–30).

In 1 Thessalonians Paul is glad to have received an encouraging report from Timothy, who has just returned from the Thessalonians (1 Thes. 3:6), and in his first letter to Timothy the young man is urged to stay on at Ephesus, where he can be most useful (1 Tim. 1:3).

When Paul writes his next letter to Timothy it is packed with the movements of Christian workers. He asks Timothy to come to him as quickly as possible, bringing Mark also, and he urgently adds, 'Do your best to get here before winter.' This is why Paul requests his cloak, which he left with Carpus in Troas, and his scrolls and notebooks. Demas has abandoned the gospel altogether and has slipped off to Thessalonica, and Paul has had to contend with Alexander the metal-worker, who 'did me a great deal of harm'. Crescens, Titus and Tychicus have moved on to Galatia, Dalmatia and Ephesus, respectively; Erastus stayed at Corinth, and poor Trophimus had to be left behind in Miletus because he was too ill to travel. Of all the leaders, only Luke is still with him. However, Paul is not entirely alone since he can send greetings from Eubulus, Pudens, Linus, Claudia 'and all the brothers'. Greetings are to be sent to Priscilla and Aquila and the household of Onesiphorus (2 Tim. 4:9–22).

That reference to Priscilla and Aquila reveals another realistic detail. They originated in Pontus but we first meet them in Corinth, when they had been driven out from Rome on the order of Emperor Claudius to expel all Jews from the city. Here in Corinth they set up business and provided a home for Paul. After eighteen months Paul travelled on to Ephesus, and this couple went with him (Acts 18). Once more they set up a church in their new home and took a young and inexperienced preacher, Apollos, under their care (Acts 18:24–26; 1 Cor. 16:19). Later they must have returned to Rome because, in his letter to that church, Paul greets them and the church meeting in their home (Rom. 16:5). However, they were soon back in Ephesus (2 Tim. 4:19). After Pontus—Rome—Corinth—Ephesus—Rome—Ephesus, Priscilla must have longed for a settled home!

Only genuine letters could weave their movements in like this; who would ever think of doing so just to create an impression? This evidence alone shows that 1 Corinthians, Romans and 2 Timothy each come from the same hand.

Tychicus will be the bearer of the letter to the Colossians and will also have with him a letter to Philemon and the runaway slave Onesimus.

The letter to the church includes greetings from Aristarchus (currently in prison with Paul), Mark, Barnabas (who is hoping to visit them soon), Jesus Justus, Epaphras, Doctor Luke and Demas (Col. 3:7–18).

The Colossians were encouraged to pass on their letter to the church at Laodicea and to read the letter Paul had sent to Laodicea (Col. 3:16). This 'missing' letter inevitably led someone to fill the gap. Our earliest copy of an epistle to the Laodiceans comes from the mid-sixth century and, as one commentator concludes, 'Of all the spurious pieces produced in the early Church, this is one of the most feeble … Comprising only twenty verses, the epistle is a pedestrian patchwork of phrases and sentences plagiarized from the genuine Pauline Epistles.'[30]

The letter to Philemon is unique among Paul's letters in that it is addressed to a specific individual and deals with only one issue. Apart from 'Apphia our sister', all the characters mentioned in this short letter— Archippus, Luke, Onesimus, Epaphras, Mark, Aristarchus and Demas— are met elsewhere in the New Testament. No serious case can be made for this letter's having been penned by anyone other than the apostle Paul. There is no reason why anyone would have invented such a letter which, unless it is genuine, would have been entirely irrelevant. However, F. C. Baur and the extreme school of German nineteenth-century critics at Tübingen denied Paul's authorship and placed it in the second century! [31] Incidentally, this is a classic case of stubborn academic prejudice on the part of critics: because Paul's letter to Philemon is associated with his letter to Colossae, and because the critics could not accept Paul as the author of Colossians, therefore his authorship of Philemon was rejected also!

All this is evidence of reliable first-century writing. No amount of clever forgery could fit the details of people, places and problems into such a collection of letters without glaring errors creeping in. These details fit perfectly with the known movements and companions of Paul recorded in the book of Acts.

---

30 Bruce M. Metzger, *The Canon of the New Testament* (Oxford: Clarendon Paperbacks, 1997), p. 183.
31 See R. J. Knowling, *The Testimony of St Paul to Christ* (1905), p. 76.

AUTHENTIC SIGNATURE

Even in his own day Paul had to warn the young churches against those he called 'false apostles' who were circulating letters bearing his name. Few of these have come down to us. Paul warned the Thessalonians against reports or letters 'supposed to have come from us' (2 Thes. 2:2). For this reason, on at least four occasions the apostle took over the stylus from his secretary and signed off the letter with his own personal signature (1 Cor. 16:21; Gal. 6:11; Col. 4:18; 2 Thes. 3:17). In fact, it would appear that this was his common practice, because to the Thessalonians he refers to it as 'the distinguishing mark in all my letters. This is how I write.'

To assume these letters are all forgeries, we must accept that the addition of Paul's signature was a masterly stroke of genius on the part of the forger of all four letters. In order to fool the early Christians he had to insert this in every one of the letters supposedly from the hand of Paul! In addition, if we are going to accept these letters as forgeries we must believe in the remarkable skill of the forger to refer in Galatians 6:11 to his large handwriting, presumably reflective of Paul's poor eyesight.

LOST LETTERS

Evidently Paul wrote many more letters than we have among the thirteen or fourteen in the New Testament. At least one letter must precede 1 Corinthians (5:9), and the letter he wrote to the church at Laodicea (Col. 4:16) is notoriously and tantalizingly lost. If a supposed letter from Paul ever comes to light in the future, the Christian church need have no fear because it will take until the end of the age for the scholars to decide whether or not it is authentic!

Part 2
The Authentic
Old Testament

Much criticism of the Bible is little more than an imposition of a preconceived position that fulfils the critic's purpose. Here are some of those critics today:

- 'The quest for the historical Moses is a futile exercise. He now belongs only to legend' (John van Seters, University of California, USA).[1]

- 'The book of Joshua is of no historical value as far as the process of settlement [in the Promised Land] is concerned' (Volkmar Fritz, University of Giessen, Germany).[2]

- 'Most scholars have abandoned the biblical text for the "patriarchal period" and the settlement of the land ... I find it difficult to discover much in the Solomon story that strikes me as likely to be historical' (Lester Grabbe, University of Hull, England).[3]

- 'The biblical narrative [of the kings of Israel] is so thoroughly filled with inconsistencies and anachronisms ... that it must be considered more of a historical novel than an accurate historical chronicle' (Israel Finkelstein, University of Tel Aviv, Israel).[4]

Without offering any evidence, Finkelstein and Silberman suggest that the details of 'Josiah's teenage religious awakening' in 2 Chronicles 34:3 'are almost certainly biographical idealizations after-the-fact'.[5] We may

---

1   The Encyclopaedia of Religion (New York: MacMillan, 1987), Vol. 10 on Moses.
2   Volkmar Fritz, 'Conquest and Settlement', in Biblical Archaeologist 2 (1987) p. 98.
3   Lester L. Grabbe, Ancient Israel: What Do We Know and How Do We Know It? (London / New York: T & T Clark, 2007), pp. 23, 114.
4   Finkelstein and Silberman, The Bible Unearthed, 175
5   Ibid., p. 275.

well ask why a teenage religious awakening is so very impossible. (The writer of this book experienced precisely that!)

In the introduction to Part 1 we noted Bishop Robinson's perception of the 'almost wilful blindness' among his fellow critical scholars (see page 15), and 'the consistent evasion by modern commentators of a solution they have already prejudged to be impossible'. That last statement is particularly significant. One Old Testament critic concedes that 'In the last years of the kings of Judah ... the biblical text can be remarkably accurate'.[6] He is compelled to this reluctant conclusion because the further the Old Testament progresses, the more archaeological evidence is available to authenticate its accuracy. In other words, the critical demand is for archaeological evidence before we can accept the accuracy of the biblical record; when there is no evidence, the biblical account will be assumed to be in error. But that overlooks the fallacy of negative proof—the idea that the absence of evidence is the evidence of absence. That mantra is both academically and logically foolish.

It is assumed among many liberal scholars that the biblical record from Abraham to Solomon was invented during the time of Josiah in the mid-seventh century BC (2 Kings 22) to create a 'history' for the nation of Judah—or possibly even later by scribes during the Persian exile (sometime in the sixth century BC) to bolster the morale of the Jews.[7] Thus David is the ideal hero, with little more historical reality than the legends surrounding St George, King Arthur or Robin Hood.

One such critic writes, 'A recent analysis of the Saul tradition finds a historical core, though this has been filtered through the distorting lenses of David's court aides, prophetic oracles, Deuteronomistic perspectives and anti-monarchical views. The stories of killing the priests of Nob or the Gibeonites are probably later calumnies [slanders].'[8] This doesn't provide much confidence in the historical reliability of the biblical record. However, there is not a shred of evidence for any of these assumptions: they are all pure hypotheses.

---

6 Grabbe, *Ancient Israel*, p. 223.
7 For example, Finkelstein and Silberman, *The Bible Unearthed*, pp. 281–284.
8 Grabbe, *Ancient Israel*, p. 112.

Professor Kenneth Kitchen concludes that the old idea of the patriarchal stories having been invented at the time of the divided monarchy at the earliest is without 'a particle of supporting factual evidence'[9]—but it is still widely assumed and taught.

1. Authentic setting

THE WORLD OF ABRAHAM

The further back we go into the history of the human race, the less archaeological confirmation of events we would expect. In time, everything disappears. Abraham takes us back to 2000 BC, and what evidence do we have for him apart from the biblical text? Directly, nothing; but indirectly, a huge amount. While to date no inscriptions from the ancient world have been discovered with a reference to Abraham, yet from the excavations of Sir Leonard Woolley in Ur of the Chaldeans during the 1920s and the discovery of thousands of documents at Mari (the ancient capital of the Amorites) the social, domestic and legal customs recorded in the book of Genesis are all well attested for this period. We will return to some of the details later.

The absence of any reference in Egyptian records to the presence of the Israelites in the land of Goshen and their escape from Egypt bothers many critics of the Bible, but it need not.

- Since the Israelites settled in the Nile delta we would hardly expect much to survive in this frequently flooded area, and proof of this is that from this area at this time 'A handful of wine-vintage dockets from broken jars is the sum total of our administrative texts so far recovered'.[10] No building above ground level has survived from this area.

- As for the escape from Egypt, no nation from the ancient world would record the loss of a huge number of slaves, the death of the firstborn across the land, and the destruction of its elite squadron of chariots.

---

9 Kenneth Kitchen, *On the Reliability of the Old Testament* (Grand Rapids: Eerdmans, 2003), pp. 188, 372.
10 Kitchen, *On the Reliability of the Old Testament*, p. 311.

But why is there no archaeological evidence of Israel's wandering in the Sinai wilderness for forty years?

One reason is that we do not know for certain which route they took across the desert, and desert nomads are known to be 'archaeologically invisible'—leaving nothing behind them. Besides, the Sinai desert has been described as 'twenty-four thousand square miles of nothing' which we have not even begun to 'dig', so it proves nothing that we have not yet discovered evidence of Israel's forty-year wandering! The episode is far too well grounded in the history of Israel to be dismissed simply because we have not yet dug up the evidence from the ground. And this is not the only account of a lost people.

According to the Greek historian Herodotus, writing four hundred years before Christ, the Persian king Cambyses II sent a 50,000-strong army to destroy the Oracle of Amun at Siwa Oasis around 524 BC. They left Egypt going into the western desert near Luxor, but the entire army was never heard of again. Theories about how they perished range from a sandstorm to an ambush, and expeditions have tried to find traces of this lost army. Similarly, the Roman Ninth Legion (*Legio IX Hispana*) was last recorded in York, England, in AD 108. Six thousand men simply disappeared from Roman records, and the theories in this case range from the simple solution of the legion having been disbanded (for which there is no record) to its total destruction by the aggressive northern tribes of Britain. But no historian doubts the existence of either the Persian or the Roman army.

We may confidently conclude with Kenneth Kitchen that the history of Israel recorded in the Old Testament 'is too closely tied to verifiable fact to be undiluted fantasy'.[11]

Before 1000 BC (the time of David) there are few references in the inscriptions of surrounding nations to Israel as a nation. There are two reasons for this.

- Until the time of Saul, Israel was not an identifiable nation under the headship of a king. This is why to date the earliest mention of Israel

---

11 Ibid., p. 462.

outside the Bible, found on a stela of Merneptah, pharaoh of Egypt and son of the great Ramesses II, describes Israel as a people group rather than as a nation occupying its own territory.[12]

- Until the time of the kings of Israel and Judah, the great empires of Assyria and later Babylonia and Persia had not risen to power and showed no presence in what we call the land of Israel; they therefore had no reason to refer to it. Even the local smaller nations, such as the Hittites, Phoenicians, Edomites, Moabites, Syrians and Philistines, left almost no mention of anyone other than themselves.

THE WORLD OF THE KINGS OF ISRAEL AND JUDAH

As the Old Testament account advances, it becomes increasingly easy to fit biblical events into a precise time frame of the Ancient Near East. When we reach the history of the divided monarchy after Solomon—the kings of Israel and Judah in our Bible—the references to those kings in the records of the surrounding nations become more and more frequent.

The following kings of Israel are referred to by name in inscriptions:

- David—by Hazael of Syria and (possibly) Mesha of Moab.

- Omri—by Mesha, king of Moab, and by Tiglath Pileser III and Shalmaneser III of Assyria.

- Ahab—by Shalmaneser III of Assyria.

- Jehu—by Shalmaneser III of Assyria.

- Jehoash—by Adad-nirari III of Assyria.

- Menahem—by Tiglath Pileser III of Assyria.

- Pekah—by Tiglath Pileser III of Assyria.

- Hoshea—by Tiglath Pileser III of Assyria.

---

12 Anderson and Edwards, *Evidence for the Bible*, p. 32. A detailed study of this can be found in Jonathan M Golden, *Ancient Canaan and Israel: An Introduction* (Oxford: Oxford University Press, 2004), p. 122; and also James K. Hoffmeier, *Israel in Egypt: The Evidence for the Authenticity of the Exodus Tradition* (Oxford: Oxford University Press, 1997), pp. 29–30.

The following kings of Judah are referred to by name in inscriptions:

- Jehoram—by Hazael of Syria.

- Ahaz—by Hazael of Syria and by Tiglath Pileser III of Assyria.

- Hezekiah—by Sennacherib of Assyria.

- Manasseh—by Esarhaddon and Ashurbanipal of Assyria.

- Jehoiachin—by Nebuchadnezzar or Amel Marduk of Babylon.

Here are a few examples of where these inscriptions actually refer to the kings of Israel or Judah:

- The king of Assyria, Shalmaneser III, records the battle of Qarqar in the sixth year of his reign, in which he claims that 'Ahab the Israelite' contributed 2,000 chariots and 10,000 infantry to the coalition of kings against him. That fixes a date firmly in 853 BC.[13]

- Shalmaneser III also records that among the many kings who sent tribute to him was 'Jehu son of Omri'. The Black Obelisk on which this is recorded is dated to the eighteenth year of Shalmaneser's reign, which gives us a date of 841 BC.[14]

- In his own records Tiglath Pileser III of Assyria refers to the assassination of Pekahiah, king of Israel (2 Kings 15:25); this was in 732 BC.[15]

In addition, many foreign kings are found mentioned by name in the biblical record in precisely the correct time and place. The following are examples of the most notable kings, but there are many more references to less significant rulers:

Pharaohs of Egypt: Shoshenq (Shishak of 1 Kings 14:25), Osorkon (So of 2 Kings 17:4), Taharqa (Tirhakah of 2 Kings 19:9), Necho (2 Kings 23:29) and Apries (Hophra of Jer. 44:30).

---

13 Anderson and Edwards, *Evidence for the Bible*, pp. 50–51.
14 Ibid., p. 52.
15 Ibid., p. 59.

Kings of Assyria: Shalmaneser V (2 Kings 17:3–4), Sargon II (Isa. 20:1) and Tiglath Pileser III (Pul in 2 Kings 15:19)

King of Moab: Mesha (2 Kings 3:4).

Kings of Syria: Ben-Hadad (1 Kings 20, and over 200 times in the Old Testament) and Hazael (1 Kings 19:15).

Kings of Babylon: Nebuchadnezzar (2 Kings 24:1, and almost 400 times in the Old Testament), and Belshazzar (Dan. 5).

An officer of Nebuchadnezzar of Babylon: Nergal-Shar-usur (Nebo-Sarsekim of Jer. 39:3).

Kings of Persia: Cyrus II (Ezra 1:1), Darius (Ezra 4:5), Xerxes (Ahasuerus of Ezra 4:6 and Esther), and Artaxerxes (Ezra 4:7).

In all, there are twenty-seven foreign kings mentioned in the biblical books of Kings and Chronicles, and all but two or three can be identified from the records of surrounding nations. As Kenneth Kitchen remarks, 'Thus we have good, mutually complementary and parallel records.'[16]

The seal impressions (known as *bullae*) of two Judaean kings, Ahaz and Hezekiah, have been recovered. In addition, *bullae* of Gedaliah and Jehukal (Jer. 38:1), Berechiah (Baruch of Jer. 45:1) and Shebna (Isa. 22:15–19) have been found.

Variation of spelling in names presents no problem: a king was often known by a different name to surrounding nations. For example, Tiglath Pileser III was known simply as Pul to the Babylonians, Greeks and Jews.

BEYOND THE EXILE

Ezra, Nehemiah and Esther, as well as the prophets Haggai, Zechariah and Malachi, are set in the period immediately after the Persian exile from 539 BC. One acknowledged expert of this period has concluded that the names (even the exact spelling), the culture, palace protocol, court

---

16 Kitchen, *On the Reliability of the Old Testament*, p. 44.

intrigues, law and language all amount to a perfect knowledge of the times and places depicted. He concludes that only a hardened unbeliever can doubt the authenticity of these records.[17]

This period of biblical history is so closely related to known events of the time that it is worth a more in-depth focus. Here are a few examples:

- At one time critics dismissed the decree of Cyrus recorded in 2 Chronicles 36:23 and Ezra 1:1–4 and 6:3–5, believing that no Persian king would have been so generous as to give permission for exiled nations to return to their homelands and rebuild their cities and temples, taking their gods with them. However, the Cyrus Cylinder, discovered by Hormuzd Rassam in 1879 among the ruins of the Marduk Temple in Babylon, does just that. Although Cyrus does not mention the Jews on this cylinder, it contains an order that perfectly mirrors the decree recorded in the Bible.

- Among the documents discovered from the Elephantine community (a fifth-century BC Jewish community at Elephantine, an island in the Nile River) is an authorization from the Persian government for the rebuilding of a temple, and the fact that a portion of the costs will be met from the royal treasury—precisely what we learn in a similar context from Ezra 6:3–4. Among these Elephantine letters are appeals very similar to that of Ezra 5:6–17.

- The Xanthos inscription, discovered in 1973, mirrors the appeal of the Jews recorded in Ezra 5–6 for permission to continue building their temple. It is now known that permission from central government was required before any temple could be built.

- Ezra 6:1–2 records that a diligent search was made of the royal archives and 'a scroll was found in the citadel of Ecbatana in the province of Media'. Persian records show that Cyrus left Babylon in the spring of 538 BC to spend the summer in Ecbatana, which is exactly where we would expect the record of the original order to be found. This was one

---

17 Yamauchi, *Persia and the Bible*, p. 237.

of four capital cities in Persia. We know also that 'royal parchments' were stored in what was called 'the fortress of the archives'.[18]

- The name Tattenai (Ezra 5:3) is found in a document dated 5 June 502 BC. In fact, all the names of Nehemiah's opponents (Sanballat, Tobiah, Geshem) are common names of this period.

- The governor of Samaria is named as 'Sanballat the Horonite' (e.g. Neh. 2:10). His governorship is confirmed by one of the Elephantine letters in which the Jews petition the governor of Judah for help and they refer to 'Delaiah and Shelemiah, the sons of Sanballat, the governor of Samaria'.[19]

- The biblical record refers to Xerxes' queen as Vashti (Esth. 1:9), while the Greek historian Herodotus calls her Amestris. It is generally accepted that this is the same name with a different pronunciation, but, as we have noted above, the use of alternative names for historic people is common both within and outside the Bible. For example, Xerxes is referred to as Ahasuerus in the Bible (e.g. Esth. 1:1); this is not an error but a Hebrew variant of the name.

- The heroic stand of the 300 Spartans at the battle of Thermopylae in the summer of 480 BC is one of the most notorious events in military history. Xerxes I led his massive Persian army, some suggest up to 100,000 strong, into Greece determined to add new territory to his empire. A delaying tactic of the Greeks was to deploy a small company of the royal bodyguard under King Leonidas to defend a 100-metre pass on the shore of the Gulf of Malia. The story of their slaughter of some 20,000 Persians in two days of relentless fighting before the Spartans were killed to all but the last man has been the stuff of books, films and legends. This costly victory for the Persians opened the way for Xerxes to send his army across Greece and destroy Athens. However, when Xerxes eventually returned home, he had still not effectively added Greece to his empire and had lost his two brothers and a large part of his army and navy.

---

18 Ibid., pp. 157–158.
19 James B. Pritchard, *Ancient Near Eastern Texts Relating to the Old Testament* (Princeton: Princeton University Press, 1969), pp. 491–492.

In addition he remembered that he had lost his queen (Esth. 2:1)! Esther 1:3 refers to the disgrace of Queen Vashti in 'the third year of his [Xerxes'] reign'. This would be 481 BC, and in that year Xerxes set out on his costly expedition to Greece. Persian records inform us that four years later he was back in Persia to proclaim his 'victory' and continue his building projects. This is the year when Esther came onto the scene 'in the seventh year of his reign' (Esth. 2:16). That four-year gap, carefully noted in Esther 1:3 and 2:16, is precisely what is required for Xerxes' four-year campaign in Greece.

- Cyrus had built a network of good roads to ensure the rapid communication of imperial decrees across his vast empire, and fast horses were bred especially for the job. The Royal Road ran from Sardis to Susa for 1,677 miles and royal couriers, changing horses and riders every twenty miles or so, could cover 240 miles in twenty-four hours and complete the journey in seven full days and nights. Herodotus wrote, 'There is nothing in the world that travels faster than these Persian couriers.' The graphic description of the couriers sent out by Xerxes recorded in Esther 8:14—'The couriers, riding the royal horses, raced out, spurred on by the king's command'—is precisely what we would expect of the express communications across the Persian Empire.

- In 1923 one commentator, Theodore Gaster, concluded that Mordecai (Esth. 2:5) was probably an invented person, because 'There is no mention anywhere but in the book of Esther of … a courtier named Mordecai who eventually replaced Haman.'[20] In 1942 the Berlin Museum published a tablet dated to the end of the reign of Darius that refers to a Mordecai, an accountant who made an inspection of Susa. Whether or not this is the same man—which is very likely—it at least confirms the name in the capital at this period. Significantly, the writer of the book of Esther invites readers to consult the official Persian records to verify the subsequent meteoric rise in the status of Mordecai (Esth. 10:2). One day those records

---

20 Theodore Gaster, *Purim and Hanukkah in Custom and Tradition* (Henry Schuman, New York, 1950), p.4, quoted in Yamauchi, *Persia and the Bible*, p.235.

may come to light. Theodore Gaster would have been wise to remember that 'the absence of evidence is not the evidence of absence'.

- Even the reference to 'the open square of the city in front of the king's gate' where Mordecai sat (Esth. 4:6) corresponds well with the details of the palace of Xerxes that was discovered in 1973.

- It had long been assumed that the Greek words and musical instruments referred to in the book of Daniel were evidence that the book was written after the conquests of Alexander the Great in the early fourth century BC. However, it is now known that trade with Greece was widespread and that at the time of Cyrus some 300 Greeks were living in the Persian court, including soldiers, sculptors, artists, architects, doctors and philosophers.[21] Oddly, some critics still use the presence of Greek words in Daniel as 'evidence' of a much later writing and therefore of the claim that it was not written in the time of the biblical Daniel.

- There is an interesting link with Israel's distant history. The statement in Esther 9:15 informing us that when the Jews were able to 'turn the tables' on their enemies throughout the Persian Empire 'they did not lay their hands on the plunder' is more significant than may immediately appear. Haman was an Agagite (3:1), which means he was a descendant of Agag the king of the Amalekites (1 Sam. 15:20). The Amalekites had been confirmed enemies of Israel from the time of Moses and Joshua (Exod. 17). Later, by sparing Agag and the best of the Amalekite goods when ordered to destroy everything, Saul lost his kingdom (1 Sam. 15:22–23). Evidently the Jews at the time of Esther, over 500 years later, had not forgotten their history and refused to touch the plunder from the defeated descendants of the Amalekites.

From before Abraham to the close of the Old Testament, the whole biblical narrative is set accurately within the historical context of each successive period. Of course this does not prove the accuracy of every statement made in the Bible, but it does demonstrate that each part of

---

21 Yamauchi, *Persia and the Bible*, pp. 379–394.

the progressive history is an authentic account of the events and people referred to. If the framework is accurately historic, then the detail adds to that. So let's turn to that now.

2. Authentic detail

Remember that it is a favourite line of Old Testament critics that the narratives of the patriarchs contain little authentic history and that the 'stories' were invented by Jewish scribes in the seventh or sixth centuries BC to provide the Jews with a history. The problem with this theory is that the Old Testament record is full of details that would have been wholly unknown to a later writer and irrelevant for a 'made-up' story. Much of the detail appears incidental or inappropriate, and certainly would not have been invented by a much later scribe. The internal evidence of the various books of the Old Testament reveals them to have been written within the time frame in which the book is set.

The social, domestic, legal, military and religious details of the earlier books of the Old Testament could never have been known by later writers, least of all invented so accurately by them. We have seen this in the New Testament era and it is even more true of the earlier period. Professor Kitchen comments that, unlike writers of fiction today, in the ancient world people did not write 'historical' novels with authentic research and background to make their accounts appear genuine.[22] Here are a few examples of authentic contemporary writing in the Bible.

- The setting of Joseph and the Israelites in Egypt is precisely what we know of the customs around 1800 BC. From inscriptions of that time, the price of a slave is known to have been 20 shekels in the time of Joseph (Gen. 37:28), but it had risen to as much as 90 shekels a thousand years later. How would a sixth-century scribe have known this?[23] Similarly, mummification and coffins (Gen. 50:3, 26) were unknown in Canaan a thousand years later when these stories were supposedly invented.

---

22 Kitchen, *On the Reliability of the Old Testament*, p. 188.
23 Hoffmeier, *Israel in Egypt*, pp. 83–84.

The details of brickmaking, taskmasters and quotas in Exodus 5 are all mirrored in Egyptian records of that time; and Moses is a known Egyptian name.

The Egyptologist James Hoffmeier concludes that details of Joseph in Egypt would have been wholly unknown to an editor 700 years later, and adds, 'It seems doubtful that a late period writer would have been interested in researching historical and cultural details simply to make the account look authentic to an audience who would not know the difference!'[24]

Just as the 'we' passages in the Acts of the Apostles pointed to the presence of Luke as an eyewitness to the events, we have something similar in the Old Testament.

• In Joshua 5:1 the writer records, 'Now when all the Amorite kings west of the Jordan and all the Canaanite kings along the coast heard how the LORD had dried up the Jordan before the Israelites until *we* had crossed over, their hearts sank and they no longer had the courage to face the Israelites' (emphasis added). That 'we' is significant. Of course, a later writer could be identifying himself with conquering Israelites, but the more natural understanding is to see in this the hand of an eyewitness to the events.

Then there are the apparently irrelevant details that certainly give colour to the narrative but appear to serve no other purpose.

• There are only three references in the Old Testament to left-handed men. They are all warriors and all Benjamites: Ehud was the judge who freed the people from the Moabites (Judg. 3:12–30); at a time of civil war Benjamin fielded 'seven hundred chosen men who were left-handed, each of whom could sling a stone at a hair and not miss' (Judg. 20:16); and David had twenty-four loyal supporters who could sling stones with either the right or the left hand (1 Chr. 12:2). The Hebrew word for 'left-

---

24 James K. Hoffmeier, *Ancient Israel in Sinai: The Evidence for the Authenticity of the Wilderness Tradition* (Oxford / New York: OUP, 2005), p. 249; and Israel in Egypt, pp. 83–95.

handed' literally means 'restricted in his right hand', and ironically the word 'Benjamin' means 'son of my right hand'. Clearly Benjamin had more than the usual percentage of left-handed warriors; whether this was genetic or taught, we cannot know, but either way it is an indication of accurate historical reporting since the writers were hardly likely to have 'imagined' that they all came from the tribe of Benjamin.

- In the lengthy list of Esau's descendants, the Edomites, the following is inserted: 'This is the Anah who discovered the hot springs in the desert while he was grazing the donkeys of his father Zibeon' (Gen. 36:24). Presumably the writer expected his contemporary readers to know exactly which 'hot springs' he was referring to and where they would be found. Even the detail that he was grazing his father's donkeys when he discovered the hot springs is a mark of authentic writing. At the risk of tedious repetition, it must be stated that this is not the kind of detail that was invented by ancient writers; it may be the mark of modern novelists, but not of writers then.

- In Deuteronomy 2, after a reference to the land of Moab, we are offered the following information: 'The Emites used to live there—a people strong and numerous, and as tall as the Anakites. Like the Anakites, they too were considered Rephaites, but the Moabites called them Emites. Horites used to live in Seir, but the descendants of Esau drove them out. They destroyed the Horites from before them and settled in their place, just as Israel did in the land the LORD gave them as their possession' (Deut. 2:10–12). We may well ask why we need to know all this. Certainly an editor writing a thousand years later could not possibly have known such detail and would have had no reason to invent it.

- Amusing, and apparently irrelevant, is the comment in Deuteronomy 3:11 that Og king of Bashan slept on a super-king-size bed, thirteen feet long, six feet wide and made of iron, and that it could still be seen in Rabbah of the Ammonites! Its relevance is precisely to authenticate a contemporary record. At the time it was a humorous marvel that was talked about far and wide. However, half a millennium later, who would either know or care about Og's bed?

- Many details find their way into the biblical text, some of which mean little to us today but were clearly intended to be understood by the first readers. The prophet Amos refers to his vision received 'two years before the earthquake, when Uzziah was king of Judah and Jeroboam son of Jehoash was king of Israel' (Amos 1:1). Amos began his ministry around 750 BC and to date we have no knowledge of this particular earthquake. Two hundred years later, Zechariah made a similar reference to this earthquake in a form that indicates it is undoubtedly the same event though clearly not a straight copy from Amos (Zech. 14:5).

- A chilling detail is added to the account of the death of Queen Jezebel. When Jehu thundered into Jezreel in his chariot, the chronicler in 2 Kings 9:30–31 records the detail of Jezebel painting her eyes and arranging her hair, which is what we would expect of this cruel and proud woman. As she looked out of the window she taunted Jehu, who had killed her husband, Ahab, as 'Zimri, you murderer of your master'. Zimri was a chariot commander who assassinated King Elah of Israel forty years earlier and then destroyed the whole royal family (1 Kings 16:9–14). This scathing and mocking jibe would not have been lost on Jehu in his chariot, bent on the murder of all seventy sons of Ahab. Although such irony would be familiar to a modern-day novelist, it was wholly unknown in the ancient world—unless it really happened.

- What may appear to be unnecessary details are scattered liberally throughout the narratives in the Old Testament. In the enthusiastic reformation under the leadership of King Hezekiah of Judah, the excessive number of sacrifices proved too much for the priests to handle and the Levites stepped up to assist. The reason that is given for the insufficient number of priests is significant and provides a detail that would never have been invented and can only have been recorded at the time: 'The priests, however, were too few to skin all the burnt offerings; so their kinsmen the Levites helped them until the task was finished and until other priests had been consecrated, for the Levites had been more conscientious in consecrating themselves than the priests had been' (2 Chr. 29:34).

3. Authentic history

EXTERNAL EVIDENCE

In the light of the ever-growing evidence of the detailed accuracy of the history recorded in the Bible, it is astounding that a Danish archaeologist and historian can still offer the naive conclusion: 'We know that the Old Testament scarcely contains historical sources about Israel's past ... It is simply an invented history with only a few referents to things that really happened or existed' (Neils Lemche, University of Copenhagen).[25]

We may wonder where Lemche has been looking. The battles, empires and rulers referred to in the Bible fit perfectly what is known from the discoveries of archaeology; seals of some of the kings and courtiers of Israel and Judah have been discovered; many of their kings are referred to in contemporary pagan inscriptions; and the culture and customs revealed in the Bible reflect accurately what is known of each successive period. Old Testament history is nowhere found to be in contradiction of known contemporary secular history. Nothing is out of place.

SENNACHERIB AND HEZEKIAH

Perhaps one of the best illustrations of this is the dramatic record of Sennacherib's invasion of Judah in the time of King Hezekiah. The events are told graphically in the biblical books in 2 Kings 18, 2 Chronicles 32 and the prophet Isaiah 36–37. Sennacherib's incursion into Judaea, his total destruction of forty-six towns and villages, including the key city of Lachish, his defeat of Egypt, which came to the rescue at Hezekiah's request, his haranguing of the leaders of Judaea at the walls of Jerusalem, and his final hasty retreat to Assyria are all equally attested in both the Assyrian and the biblical records. Nothing is in conflict, even to the detail of Sennacherib recording that he shut up Hezekiah in Jerusalem 'like a bird in a cage'.[26]

In spite of all this careful detail in both records, one critic writes of the 'embellishment' in the biblical version of events when the Bible records

25 Niels Peter Lemche, *BAR*, July/Aug 2000, p. 16.
26 The 'Taylor Prism'. See Anderson and Edwards, *Evidence for the Bible*, p. 75.

the loss of the Syrian army in one night (2 Kings 19); he makes this claim merely because there is no such reference in Assyrian records. Nor would we expect there to be. Our critic must know that ancient nations did not record their own disastrous defeats. However, we may well ask why Sennacherib hastily withdrew from Jerusalem and, according to his own records, left it as the only capital city in all his campaigns that remained intact with its king inside. Besides, the ancient Greek historian Herodotus also records the destruction of the Assyrian siege forces in one night, though admittedly he attributed it to a plague of mice that gnawed its way through the Assyrian equipment, rather than to the hand of God!

Unfortunately, for many archaeologists and historians of the biblical record, unreliability is something that is consistent with their own preconceived views. Therefore the consistent agreement of the two records of the Sennacherib/Hezekiah conflict is set aside simply because the biblical record adds a detail about which the Assyrian inscriptions are silent, exactly as we would expect them to be.

'TO THIS DAY'

A small but significant phrase occurs around fifty times in the Bible. 'To this day' is used to refer to a town name that was changed and was still in use at the time of writing, a site of special religious significance, a people whose status or location had changed, or some event that was memorable in the history of Israel. In every case the phrase implies that the place, people or marker was still present. This is evidence of the record having been written close to the actual time.

There are at least nine markers for sites of significance in Israel that were still visible in the writers' day: Rachel's tomb (Gen. 35:20); the monument for the crossing of the Jordan (Josh. 4:9); the pile of stones over Achan's grave (Josh. 7:26); the cave of the five entombed kings (Josh. 10:27); Gideon's altar at Ophrah (Judg. 6:24); the rock commemorating the return of the ark (1 Sam. 6:18); Absalom's monument (2 Samuel 18:18); the Field of Blood (Matt. 27:8); and the tomb of David (Acts 2:29). In addition there are some fifteen changed place names where the new name was still used 'to this day'. These are examples of a near-contemporary recording of the events.

If the books of Joshua and Samuel were invented by a scribe in the sixth century, over eight hundred years after Joshua, these piles of stone were most unlikely to have survived the inevitable time and weather erosion. 'Listed buildings' were unknown then. We know how quickly whole cities of the past were buried under the sands. The vast city of Nineveh was destroyed by Babylon in 612 BC; the 'palace without equal'—with its eighty rooms, library of 20,000 clay tablets and seven miles of city walls—crumbled into the desert and within two hundred years virtually nothing above ground was visible. It remained like this until the archaeologist Austin Henry Layard discovered it in 1847.

Walk around a cemetery today and try to read the nineteenth-century inscriptions, and then imagine how much will still be there in eight hundred years! Many of the wartime defences built across England between 1939 and 1945 have virtually disappeared under the ground after less than eighty years.

Why would a scribal novelist have invented monuments and claimed that they were still visible when anyone could check out the lie?

- The reference in 1 Samuel 6:18 to the large rock on which the ark of the covenant was placed when it was returned by the Philistines 'is a witness to this day in the field of Joshua of Beth Shemesh'. The directions are very specific, and anyone is invited to go down to the field of Joshua of Beth Shemesh and inspect it. This would be around 1000 BC. The same is said of the monument erected by Absalom in his own honour: 'It is called Absalom's Monument to this day' (2 Sam. 18:18).

- Joshua 8:26–28 is sometimes used to demonstrate a supposed contradiction in Scripture. Joshua destroyed the city of Ai and 'made it a permanent heap of ruins, a desolate place to this day'. However, by the return from exile in 539 BC, men who had been exiled in the time of Nebuchadnezzar (586 BC) went back to their home towns, including men from 'Bethel and Ai'. This is clear evidence that Joshua was not written at the time of the return from exile but within a generation or so of the actual event. What happened was this: Joshua destroyed the city of Ai and *intended* it to be a permanent ruin, which it remained for some time. However, by the time of the Babylonian conquest eight hundred years later, the city had been rebuilt. No sixth-century scribe would have invented Joshua 8:28 when he knew that the city had been rebuilt.

- Joshua 15:63 records that in their conquest of the promised land of Canaan, Judah could not dislodge the Jebusites, who were living in Jerusalem, and that 'to this day the Jebusites live there with the people of Judah'. Evidently, even though the men of Judah later 'put the city to the sword and set it on fire' (Judg. 1:8), the Jebusites held on and the Benjamites, who were part of Judah, were compelled to live alongside them (Judg. 1:21). Therefore, there is no so-called 'anachronism' in 1 Samuel 17:54 when the young boy David is said to have taken the head of Goliath to Jerusalem. At this time the city was still occupied by both Jebusites and Benjamites and it would have been natural for him to take his trophy of war to the king's own tribe—the Benjamites. Gradually, the Jebusites appear to have ousted the Benjamites and closed the gates against David when he finally determined to take full possession of the city (1 Chr. 11:4–9). Joshua and Judges must have been written long before David finally captured the city or else the claim in Judges that the Jebusites held on to it would have been not meaningless but ridiculous.

- Rahab, the woman who concealed the spies and was rewarded with her life and that of her family after the fall of Jericho, 'lives among the Israelites to this day' (Josh. 6:25); this is not a reference to her descendants, but to Rahab herself.

- When Solomon brought the ark of the covenant into Jerusalem so that it could be housed in the newly built temple, an intriguing detail is added: the carrying poles that fitted into the four corner rings were so long that their ends could be seen protruding from the Holy Place in front of the inner sanctuary; then follows the significant phrase 'and they are still there today' (1 Kings 8:8). That is a detail that could never have been added after 587 BC, when the Babylonians totally destroyed the temple in Jerusalem; nothing more is known of the ark from this date. Only a fool, or a brilliant forger unlike any ancient writer of history, would have added a detail like this once the temple had been destroyed.

- In 1 Kings 12:19 (also 2 Chr. 10:19) the reader is reminded that from the time of the division of the monarchy, when Jeroboam took the ten northern tribes (Israel) and left Solomon's son, Rehoboam, with only the tribes of Benjamin and Judah, 'Israel has been in rebellion against the house of David to this day'. In the year 722 BC, the northern territory of Israel was conquered and dispersed by Assyria and ceased to exist as a separate nation. After this date, two hundred years before the supposed scribal forger in the mid-sixth century, Israel could not have been in rebellion against Judah because Israel simply did not exist as a nation.

MANY MORE BOOKS

It is evident that there were numerous official records, to which we now have no access, detailing events recorded in the Bible. At least ten are mentioned in the Old Testament if we exclude those that may refer to books within the Bible; for example, in 1 Chronicles 29:29 the 'records of Samuel the seer' most likely refers to the biblical books of 1 and 2 Samuel; and the 'book of the kings of Judah and Israel' (2 Chr. 16:11; 27:7; 32:32) is probably 1 and 2 Kings in the Bible.

- The first of the 'lost' books is referred to in Numbers 21:14, where 'the Book of the Wars of the LORD' is quoted.

- Joshua 10:13 dipped into the 'Book of Jashar' (possibly meaning 'the just' or 'upright') for some of the details of the extraordinary long day in the battle for Gibeon. King David apparently added some verses to this same book of poetry in his lament for the deaths of Saul and Jonathan in battle (2 Sam. 1:17–27). That is all we know of the book.

- The life of David is recorded for us in the 'records of Samuel the seer' (1 Chr. 29:29) which, as we have seen, probably refers to the books of Samuel in the Bible. However, in this and the next verse it is evident that there were also the 'records of Nathan the prophet and the records of Gad the seer, together with the details of his reign and power, and the circumstances that surrounded him and Israel and the kingdoms of all the other lands'. Some of this may have been included in our books of Samuel and Kings, but evidently there is much more that we do not have, including whatever was written in 'the book of the annals of King David' (1 Chr. 27:24). Israel was anxious to ensure that the details of the reign of its great king were left for posterity.

- There is good evidence that the book of Proverbs really does contain many of the wise sayings of King Solomon. Proverbs 25:1 records that these additional proverbs of Solomon were 'copied by the men of Hezekiah king of Judah'. This is exactly what we would expect from the period of spiritual revival under Hezekiah; he would have been anxious to gather the wisdom of the renowned Solomon, and there would have been no reason for a statement like this to have been included if it were not true. There would doubtless be more to learn about Solomon's reign and the 'wisdom he displayed' if we could find the 'annals of Solomon' referred to in 1 Kings 11:41.

- Esther 10:2 informs us that in 'the book of the annals of the kings of Media and Persia' there is much more about Xerxes and about Mordecai as well. We noted in the chapter on 'Authentic Setting' that a tablet in the Berlin Museum, dated around the end of the reign of Darius, refers to a Mordecai, an accountant who made an inspection of Susa; he may be our man (see page 56). One day these missing records may come to light.

There are a few more examples but these are sufficient to illustrate the contemporary nature of the biblical books. No writer in Bible times would even have imagined inventing a few unknown books in order to give some kind of realism to his work.

In addition to this, any reader who has worked his or her way through the two books of Kings in the Old Testament and reached the two books of Chronicles will quickly discover that many accounts are duplicated, though few are identical. Remember that the two essential legal principles in a case are:

The number of independent witnesses confirms the greater likelihood of the accuracy of their report. And the agreement of their evidence significantly enhances the truth of their record.

The reliability of a report is confirmed by the degree to which details match known events and circumstances.

In the first place, two non-contradictory accounts must reinforce the authenticity of the history recorded; in addition, so much of the historical detail is matched by what we know of the period of the monarchy in Israel and Judah. If, where the evidence can be tested, it is found to be accurate—which it is again and again—then we have every right to claim that the detail which cannot be matched by contemporary pagan records must also be presumed accurate. That is an essential legal approach to any document, ancient or modern.

4. Authentic honesty

If those sixth-century scribes were out to bolster the morale of the Jews by providing them with a glorious history and David as a great hero, they made a very poor job of it.

The patriarchs are revealed as men of weakness: Abraham lied to save his skin and Jacob deceived his blind and ageing father. Moses, the heroic leader out of slavery, lost his temper. The Israelites in the wilderness proved to be a rabble of disobedient grumblers, and once settled in the Promised Land were often no better. Judges is a disheartening book to read, with Israel sinking to its lowest ebb, and Samson was hardly a boyhood hero whose morality should be copied. Saul was a disaster as the first king of Israel, building a monument to himself and finally attending a seance for guidance.

The great hero David brought discredit on his God, himself, and his nation by adultery and murder. Besides, if the story of David is a legend, we would expect that he would be the king responsible for building the first temple in Jerusalem. In the event his son was, but even the wise and powerful Solomon committed apostasy towards the end of his life.

All this is hardly a catalogue of glory to inspire a people in exile!

To read 2 Kings 17:7–23 is to read a miserable litany of unfaithfulness throughout the history of Israel; one wonders why these accounts were not 'filtered out' by all those supposed editors.

The honesty of Old Testament narrative is unique in ancient writing. All that is bad is faithfully recorded: military losses and moral failures. By contrast, in the ancient world it was rare for bad things to be reported unless they happened to an enemy. As late as the Roman Empire it was common for inscriptions of an emperor, his family or a high official to be obliterated if they fell from favour. Caracalla, the emperor from AD 211 to 217 and acknowledged as 'one of the most bloodthirsty tyrants in Roman history', erased all references to his wife, Plautilla, and his brother, Geta, after he had arranged their murders. The same happened to Nero and Domitian when they fell from power. Anything bad and anyone disgraced were erased from the records. The practice was known as *damnatio memoria*—the damnation of memory. For the ancient world, if a name was erased or even a face hacked out, that person ceased to exist.

This, of course, is nothing new; even today's leaders and historians have a habit of ignoring that which they wish had never happened!

5. Authentic religion

One of the most significant evidences of Old Testament history as a unique revelation is the way it stands apart from the collective views of Ancient Near Eastern literature. Of course there are some similarities, such as the widespread belief in ancient literature of a global flood, and there are a few similarities between the temple of Solomon and pagan or Egyptian temples, and between the laws of Hammurabi and those of Moses; but more significant are the beliefs revealed in the Hebrew Scriptures that bear no resemblance to the beliefs of the surrounding nations. How do we account for this apart from revelation? To suggest that Israel's religion was little more than a development from their surrounding influences is completely to ignore the wide contrasts.[27]

---

27 For a detailed analysis of the difference between Israel and the Ancient Near East, see John H. Walton, *Ancient Near Eastern Thought and the Old Testament: Introducing the Conceptual World of the Hebrew Bible* (Nottingham: IVP Apollos, 2007).

• From the beginning, Israel's religion was monotheistic—a belief in one God alone to the exclusion of all others. This was the first command of Israel's law (Exod. 20:3). By contrast, all the religions of the ancient world boasted a multitude of gods who each had its part to play even when some were seen to be above the others. Ishtar, for example, was 'goddess of goddesses';[28] and equally of Shamash, the sun god, it was written that 'no one among the gods is equal to thee'.[29]

There have been attempts to suggest that the monotheism of Moses was influenced by the brief monotheism of Egyptian Pharaoh Amenhotep IV, who changed his name to Akhenaten in honour of what he considered to be the only god, Aten. However, his idea of the Aten god was vastly different from the God revealed to Moses. Besides this, any suggested link fails if we accept the most likely date for Moses' birth—around 1526 BC, nearly two hundred years before Amenhotep came to the throne of Egypt in 1352!

• Israel's understanding of the character of God was so different from the character of the nations' gods. Their gods came into being (known as 'theogony'), whereas Israel's God was eternal. The gods were fallible, emotional (good and bad), procreative and physical. And they could be incompetent. They could be crafty, deceptive, lustful, even hungry. They had needs that were met by their worshippers. For this reason an idol was 'awakened in the morning, washed, clothed, fed two sumptuous meals each day (while music was played in its presence), and put to bed at night'.[30] The idea of the gods as just, faithful, wise, good or gracious was not dominant. They acted as they did through no necessary moral incentive. Typically, the Hittites saw their gods as needing to be fed and flattered, and capable of 'behaviour which we would consider unseemly or at least undignified'.[31] They were unreliable and capable of error—which their worshippers would point out to them.

---

28 A prayer of Ammiditana of Babylon (c.1600 BC) to Ishtar the goddess of fertility and love. Pritchard, *Ancient Near Eastern Texts*, p. 383.
29 A prayer of Ashurbanipal of Assyria (668–633 BC) to the sun god Shamash. Ibid., p. 387.
30 Ibid., p. 136.
31 O. R. Gurney, *The Hittites* (London: Penguin , 1975), p. 157.

- The relationship between Israel and their God, who as a Father entered into a covenant with them to care for them in return for their obedience to his detailed moral and ceremonial laws, was unknown among the surrounding religions. For their part, the gods were not bound by any covenant relationship with their devotees.

- Although the gods were not restricted to a geographical area and could extend their area from their base where they were worshipped, they were, however, limited in their sphere of control. Gods could be multiplied ad infinitum and there was no concept of true versus false gods: only those more effective or more powerful than others. And because there was no covenant relationship with the gods, orthodoxy and heresy were virtually unknown. The nearest to heresy was the attempt by Amenhotep IV in fourteenth-century Egypt to exalt Aten above all others. A traveller could worship the gods of the nation he was visiting and this was not seen as disloyalty to his gods at home. By contrast, for example, at the dedication of the temple in Jerusalem, Solomon expressed his exalted view of Israel's God in a way beyond the understanding of the devotees of the pagan gods: 'Will God really dwell on earth with men? The heavens, even the highest heavens, cannot contain you. How much less this temple that I have built!' (2 Chr. 6:18).

- The gods of the Ancient Near East had to be worshipped in the form of an idol. If there was no idol, the spirit of the god could not be there. Similarly, consulting the stars, divination in various forms, and checking the world of the spirits were all part of the normal religions of the Ancient Near East. For Israel, idolatry was an abomination and all forms of divination and necromancy were outlawed (Deut. 5:7–8; 18:9–14). Charms and household gods were an accepted part of the religions surrounding Israel. These were all forbidden to Israel. Significantly, the dung (scarab) beetle, of which images, charms and amulets are found everywhere in the Ancient Near East (and especially in Egypt), is never even mentioned in the Old Testament.

- The details of the tabernacle and later the temple in Jerusalem are not mirrored in any Ancient Near Eastern documents. If the nations asked Israel, 'Why is it all like this?' the answer would be, 'Because our God commanded it this way.' However, the Messianic significance of those details is increasingly revealed throughout the Old Testament. By contrast, the significance of pagan rituals is never revealed, even if they had any.

• Nothing similar to a Sabbath observance has ever been found in Ancient Near Eastern religion. Although the concept of rest among the gods (even after creating) is not new, nowhere is the pattern transferred to mankind. In Egypt, Israel had been used to a ten-day week, and although the Sumerians and Babylonians used a seven-day week, the weekly cycle of six days and a Sabbath day had been fixed in Israel's religion long before the Babylonians came onto the scene.

• While the gods were seen as powerful and even omnipotent—the moon god Sin, for example, is 'decider of the destinies of heaven and earth … whose word no one alters'[32] —none of them shared this gift alone, and many vied with each other for the ultimate authority.

• The system of sacrifices for total forgiveness was unknown among all Israel's neighbours. They had no concept of forgiveness such as David expressed in, for example, Psalms 32:5 and 51:17, or experienced by Manasseh in 2 Chronicles 33:13. There are pleas for the deity to turn away his or her anger, and even an admission of guilt, but there is no sense of having been forgiven. The sacrifices were more to satisfy the gods than to cleanse the worshippers from personal guilt. Similarly, adherence to the ceremonial was all-important, whereas for Israel the ceremony without an accompanying holy life was unacceptable (Isa. 1:13; Amos 5:23). Holiness in the Ancient Near East was more to do with adherence to the cultic ritual than moral integrity. While right and wrong were understood in terms of what was good for society,[33] this was not related to the character of the gods. On the contrary, for Israel,

---

32 A prayer of Ashurbanipal of Assyria (668–633 BC) to the moon god Sin. Pritchard, *Ancient Near Eastern Texts*, p. 386.

33 See, for example, Ashurbanipal's prayer to the sun god. Pritchard, *Ancient Near Eastern Texts*, p. 387.

moral uprightness was defined precisely by the character of God. 'Be holy, because I am holy' (Lev. 11:45) was an unknown concept to the surrounding nations.

- There are creation accounts from the Ancient Near East, just as there are accounts of a global flood. However, whereas the latter often show similarities with the Genesis record—such as the Sumerian, Atrahasis and Gilgamesh epics, which reflect a widespread knowledge of a terrifying global disaster—the creation accounts show almost no correspondence with the biblical account. There are no accounts of an original human pair who became the ancestors of the entire human race. Apart from the Egyptian pharaoh bearing the image of the gods, there is no concept of the human race having been created in the image of the Creator. Similarly, in these other creation accounts the human race was created to serve the gods and provide food for them, undertaking the work the gods disdained. By contrast, Israel's God provided food for his people.

- Israel understood their laws, and indeed their history, as part of the covenant that the only true God had given to the people by divine revelation. This was unknown to the surrounding nations. For this reason the history of Israel is a coherent development in which each stage moves the nation towards an ultimate goal—the appearance of their Messiah, promised at the very outset of creation (Gen. 3:15). The long-term prophecies of the Old Testament prophets, which could reach forward many centuries, are unknown in the literature of the Ancient Near East.

- As for the afterlife, the Egyptians were exceptional in their view of the dead. The Book of the Dead and the Pyramid spells are detailed accounts of the progress of the soul beyond death. However, there is little confidence that anyone will eventually reach the happy land somewhere in the far west and escape the jaws of Ammut, the crocodile-headed monster. For the rest of the Ancient Near East there was even less certainty regarding the future. The theme of a Messiah who would one day rescue a chosen people and recreate this ruined world, a theme that runs throughout the more than two-thousand-year history of the biblical narrative, is found nowhere in the literature of the Ancient Near East.

ANCIENT LAW CODES

Ancient law codes are not unknown—there are at least six in Ancient Near Eastern literature—but their contrasts with the laws given to Moses are significant. One of the earliest is the Code of Ur-Nammu, which is dated to around the time of Abraham (c.2000 BC). Only thirty-two laws survive, and, as we would expect, they deal with the same areas of human relationships (though almost exclusively with sex, violence and theft) as those given to Moses. Beyond this, there are few comparisons to be made.

More interesting is the law code of Hammurabi, a king of Babylon who lived between Abraham and Moses. It has been suggested that Moses based his laws on Hammurabi's; however, there is no evidence for this. Of the 282 laws of Hammurabi, those with a close similarity to the Mosaic laws amount to fewer than twenty. Many more cover the same areas of human relationships as we would expect, but a comparison highlights the differences more than the similarities. The contrasts are significant:

- The laws of Hammurabi address many gods—at least nine and possibly as many as fifteen. Moses knows only one.

- Hammurabi presents his laws *to* the gods. Moses received his as a revelation *from* God.

- In Hammurabi's laws, the exalted reputation and wisdom of the king is constantly in focus. Moses received no credit for the laws of God.

- The laws of Hammurabi have no reference to the moral qualities of the gods. The Mosaic laws are a reflection of the holiness of God.

- There are clear rules for the punishment of crimes in the laws of Hammurabi, but there is no provision of forgiveness, since the gods are not interested in morality. For the Mosaic laws, sin is primarily an affront to the character of God.

It has been suggested that Hammurabi and others were not lawgivers or even lawmakers: they merely presented case history. In the Old Testament the Mosaic laws were fixed throughout the long history of Israel, and subsequent kings were expected to copy them out (Deut. 17:18–19). There is nothing in Ancient Near Eastern literature to compare with the Decalogue (the Ten Commandments) for simplicity, conciseness and relevance.

Such a diversity of contrasts between the religion of Israel and the religions of the nations of the Ancient Near East—all close neighbours to Israel—must surely leave us with the question as to why and how Israel was so very different. One thing is plain: Israel did not 'borrow' its religion and laws from its neighbours; its religion and laws are uniquely different. So how did it get them? The most satisfactory explanation is that which the Old Testament itself claims: Israel's religion was revealed by God through his servants the prophets.

6. Authentic geography

Unlike most foundational books of world religions, the Hebrew Scriptures are packed with place names and routes taken. Two of the most obvious are the route of the exodus, when Israel left Egypt and moved out into the Sinai desert, and the division of the land of Canaan among the twelve tribes.

The route taken by the Israelites is recorded in careful detail in Numbers 33. Fifty different place names are documented in sequence. Clearly this is intended to be an accurate record of the precise route taken by the Israelites during their forty years in the wilderness. Unfortunately we have no way of knowing where many of these places are today, which is hardly surprising 3,500 years later and considering how often modern cities have changed their names in a far shorter period of time. Sixteen hundred years ago the Romans left Britain and many of their city names are unrecognizable by most people today: for example, Caesaromagus (Chelmsford), Camulodunum (Colchester), Duroliponte (Cambridge) and Venta Belgarum (Winchester).

These wilderness place names are evidence of an authentic record carefully noted by someone who travelled with Israel through the desert at that time. There is no parallel in ancient writing for an invented list of non-existent places simply to give the appearance of authenticity.

Similarly, the book of Joshua includes the details of the geographical boundaries between the various tribes. While chapter 13 lists the land still to be taken, chapters 15 through to 19 reveal the full inventory of towns allotted to each tribe. Take, for example, the allotment for the tribe of Judah. This is part of it from Joshua 15:

Their southern boundary started from the bay at the southern end of the Salt Sea, crossed south of Scorpion Pass, continued on to Zin and went over to the south of Kadesh Barnea. Then it ran past Hezron up to Addar and curved around to Karka. It then passed along to Azmon and joined the Wadi of Egypt, ending at the sea. This is their southern boundary. The eastern boundary is the Salt Sea as far as the mouth of the Jordan. The northern boundary started from the bay of the sea at the mouth of the Jordan, went up to Beth Hoglah and continued north of Beth Arabah to the Stone of Bohan son of Reuben … The boundary ended at the sea. The western boundary is the coastline of the Great Sea (vv. 2–6, 11-12).

As with the exodus route from Egypt, we cannot be certain where all these places are, but it is hardly likely that anyone would have invented such details simply to make the settlement look genuine. Besides, adherence to these boundaries apparently stood the test of time, since we do not find the twelve tribes squabbling over boundary issues.

7. Authentic genealogies, chronologies and numbers

Few readers of the Bible laboriously articulate the long lists of names in genealogies or the records of numbers. However, the Bible is full of genealogies and chronologies, so they must be important. Years ago Edwin Thiele concluded, 'Without chronology it is not possible to understand history, for chronology is the backbone of history.'[34] We might add that from a biblical perspective genealogy is just as important. What makes the Bible so authentic and reliable is that it is full of both chronology and

---

34 Edwin R. Thiele, *A Chronology of the Hebrew Kings* (Grand Rapids: Zondervan, 1977), p. 7.

genealogy. Unlike almost all the sacred literature of so many of the world religions, you can check the Bible against the history and known figures of its times. It is much more than a history book, but it is nevertheless a book of history.

THOUSANDS OF NAMES!

The book of Genesis lays the foundation for something that is very significant for the subsequent history of Israel: the importance of genealogies. Although in recent years among Western societies there has been an increased interest in tracing one's family, for most of us, generally speaking, it doesn't much matter who our great-great-great-grandfather was. But that was not so in Bible times. A genealogy was a vital part of every man's credentials. It was as important to him as our passport is to us.

This is precisely why the Old Testament in particular is full of genealogies—lists of names tracing the line back for many generations. And that is also why we have two independent genealogies of Jesus in Matthew and Luke, Matthew following the line of descent through Joseph, and Luke, through Mary.[35] Genealogies were vitally important credentials.

We may find the lists of names in the Old Testament tedious reading, but they are there for a purpose. There are more genealogies in Numbers, Ezra and Nehemiah, and the first nine chapters of 1 Chronicles contain little more than the genealogies of a few thousand men and women. Nobody made up a genealogy; each was recorded accurately and stored carefully. Genealogies were part of a family history, not of legend or wishful imagination. In fact, reliable men, such as Shemaiah and Iddo, were specifically entrusted to 'deal with genealogies' (2 Chr. 12:15).

The first detailed genealogy occurs as early as the fifth chapter of Genesis. But what is important for us to understand is this: genealogies were expected to be accurate records. The whole book of Genesis contains a detailed genealogy of the early history of the human race in general and of the nation of Israel in particular—and it mattered that it could be relied upon.

---

35 The debate about whether or not Matthew traces the genealogy through Joseph and Luke through Mary is detailed. A summary of the discussion can be found in William Hendriksen's commentary on Luke 3:23–38 in *Luke* (Edinburgh: Banner of Truth, 1979), pp. 221–225.

In the ancient world genealogies, or what we might call family trees, were essential to establish a rightful claim to the throne, a genuine tribal connection or a legitimate ministry as a priest. The importance of the last is seen, for example, in Ezra 2:59, 62 (and repeated in Neh. 7:61–65) when the Jews returned to Jerusalem from exile around the year 458 BC. Two groups are mentioned who had somehow lost their family records during the exile. The first group could not show that their families were descended from Israel, and the second group were priests but, having searched for their family records and been unable to find them, they were excluded from officiating as priests. We might suggest that both groups should simply go away and 'invent' a long genealogy, but that would never have been done. Even these two insertions into a long chapter of numbers and genealogies are evidence of an authentic record; no editor would make up these exceptions if the whole record was not an accurate transcription of the various family groups. For his part, Ezra the priest could trace his genealogy right back to Aaron the son of Moses (Ezra 7:1–5).

This has implications for all the genealogies, and especially for those in the early chapters of Genesis. It has been suggested that the genealogies in Genesis 10–11 are conflated and that we could insert many generations between one name and the next. It is perfectly true that sometimes genealogies are reduced by missing out many family members between one name and the next. Kenneth Kitchen writes, 'Within Hebrew and related traditions, such "official" father-to-son sequences can represent the actual facts of life or they can be a condensation from an originally longer series of generations.'[36] However, one thing is clear: they were not invented.

On the other hand, in these chapters there are two indications that the generations are complete. The first is the detail in chapter 10 of each father and son; there is no space for 'missing' generations. In chapter 11 the unbroken line is even clearer since the age is given of each father before the birth of the firstborn son. And in case we assume that it may simply

---

36 Kitchen. *On the Reliability of the Old Testament*, p. 440.

mean that 'A fathered the line culminating in B',[37] we are given the year in which he died after the birth of B.

Interestingly, the genealogy of Israel (Jacob) in Genesis 46 gives us the names of the mothers of each of the grandchildren and apparently irrelevant details along the way: one was a 'son of a Canaanite woman' (v. 10); two 'died in the land of Canaan' (v. 12); three were born to Leah 'in Paddan Aram' along with their sister Dinah (v. 15); another group have their sister Serah slipped into the list (v. 17).

Some of the details in the genealogies may seem entirely irrelevant for us, but their inclusion helps to authenticate the lists; it was not the practice of the Israelites to invent such details simply to add interest to their records. The genealogies had a serious, not merely a literary, purpose.

- A glance through the list in Nehemiah 3, for example, illustrates this point well: verse 5 laments that some of the leaders 'would not put their shoulders to the work under their supervisors'; verse 12 adds the detail that Shallum repaired a section of the wall 'with the help of his daughters'; while verse 30 informs us that Meshullam 'made repairs opposite his living quarters' and verse 32 comments that even the 'goldsmiths and merchants' joined the work gang. There are many more such details.

- 1 Chronicles 7:21–22 provides an intriguing family detail of a spat between two sons of Ephraim and the 'native-born men of Gath' which led to the death of the sons, the comfort of the neighbours to the grieving father, the birth and naming of his next-born son, and even the record of his daughter who was in the construction industry! This apparently superfluous information points to an accurate historical record.

- The detailed care in recording these chronologies is revealed in an apparent aside in 1 Chronicles 26:10. The chronicler is careful to note that Hoash had a number of sons and that although Shimri was not the firstborn 'his father had appointed him the first'. This is a small detail in an extensive list of those David allocated for the future temple services.

---

37 As Kitchen suggests, ibid., p. 441.

Evidently the meticulous chronicler around 1000 BC was familiar with the family hierarchy and guarded against the suggestion that he had made a mistake here, since Shimri was not the firstborn. Effectively he informs us, 'I know Shimri was not the firstborn, but his father changed the rules in this case.'

8. Authentic official records

Although most of the Old Testament was written in Hebrew, there are a small number of passages recorded in Aramaic. In the book of Ezra we have some Persian records that are quoted. These were originally documented in Aramaic, which was widely the common language at that time (the lingua franca), just as Greek was in New Testament times. In Ezra 4:8–6:18 and 7:12–26 there are decrees and correspondence sent between the kings of Persia (Cyrus II, Darius I and Artaxerxes I) and officials in Judah. This correspondence would almost certainly have been carried out in Aramaic, and, rather than translate it into Hebrew, Ezra decided to keep it in the original official language, knowing that his readers could handle this as easily. This is an indication of the accuracy of the text in passing on the official correspondence verbatim.

Alongside the conviction that the Bible was 'God-breathed' via the minds of the human writers (2 Tim. 3:16; 2 Peter 1:21), it is understood that many of the recorders of history in the Bible made use of official records and, as we have seen, this included family records (genealogies). No one supposes that these lengthy lists of names were revealed directly by God into the minds of the writers.

9. Authentic evidence

Some of the items in this section have been covered earlier in this book; however, they are included here to complete a summary of a few of the main evidences.

The wildly exaggerated comments of some scholars are incredible in the light of the growing amount of evidence from the world of archaeology.

The reality is that nothing from archaeological discovery has indisputably demonstrated the inaccuracy of the biblical record. On the contrary, 'archaeology, correctly understood, always confirms the accuracy of the Bible' (Professor Donald Wiseman, late professor of Assyriology, University of London).[38]

It must be remembered that the most archaeology can do is to comment on the biblical narrative by providing evidence as to whether or not the incident is likely to have taken place; it can say nothing about the significance of the story. What archaeology can rarely do is to claim that an event did not happen or that a person did not exist; it can only conclude that we have not yet found the archaeological evidence for such an event or such a person. To claim otherwise is what we have seen as 'the fallacy of negative proof'.

No archaeologist can assert, 'There was no David and there was no Goliath; therefore, the story of David and Goliath is legend.' Equally, speaking only as an archaeologist or historian, someone cannot claim that there was a David who killed Goliath. However, what he or she can say is that we now have indisputable archaeological evidence for a dynasty of David and that the name Goliath (if not referring to the same man) was known in Gath at the time David fought with the giant.[39] Beyond that, we either believe the episode recorded in the Bible or we don't; but at least we can claim that everything in the account fits perfectly with what we do know of that time.

It is significant that from the time of the divided monarchy (when ten tribes under Jeroboam I established the nation of Israel and left two tribes under Rehoboam in Judah), critical archaeologists take the biblical record more seriously. The reason is that for this period there is far more positive archaeological evidence to authenticate the biblical record.

Many times the Bible has been assumed to be in error, only to be found accurate after new archaeological discoveries. A few examples are given

---

38 From a personal conversation.
39 The Tel Dan inscription, discovered in 1993, is one of at least two inscriptions that authenticate the name David as that of a king in Israel (see paragraph 'David of Judah' below). In 2005 a team under Professor Aren Maeir of Bar-Llan University discovered at Tel es-Safi (biblical Gath) a Philistine inscription containing the name Goliath.

here, but the reader is encouraged to read *Evidence for the Bible* [40] for an accessible introduction to the many archaeological finds that authenticate the biblical record.

DAVID OF JUDAH: THE DYNASTY THAT NEVER WAS?

No evidence of David the king of Israel had ever been found outside the Bible; it was therefore assumed by some that his story was merely a legend made up by Jewish scribes sometime after the sixth century BC to bolster the morale of the Jews in exile. In July 1993 a broken basalt inscription was found at Tel Dan in Northern Israel. It caused massive interest in the world of archaeology because the Tel Dan Inscription is unquestionably dated to around 796 BC and it refers to 'The House of David'. This means that the dynasty of King David was known around 250 years before the legends of David were supposedly made up by Jewish scribes. Critical scholars now concede that David was, at the very least, a real person.

SARGON OF ASSYRIA: THE KING WHO NEVER LIVED?

Until 1843 the only known reference to Sargon was found in Isaiah 20:1, where Sargon is named as the king of Assyria. It was therefore assumed by some academics that no such king had ever existed. However, in 1843 the French archaeologist Paul-Emil Botta uncovered the great city of Khorsabad in modern-day Iraq. It was identified as the fortress city of Sargon and included his palace and library. Sargon is now one of the best-known Assyrian kings, and is understood to have been one of the most powerful rulers in the ancient world.

Equally significant is the fact that in the Bible the Hebrew text of Sargon's name contains precisely the same consonants as those found in Assyrian texts, unlike the Babylonian spelling of the name. If the biblical writers were compiling these accounts in the fifth or sixth centuries BC, by which time the Assyrian dialect had long since ceased to be used, how would they have known the correct spelling unless they had had access

---

40 Anderson and Edwards.

to eighth-century Assyrian records? The more likely explanation is that Isaiah was written at the time of the events described.

BELSHAZZAR OF BABYLON: THE BANQUET THAT WAS NEVER HELD?

Daniel chapters 5, 7 and 8 claim that there was a king in Babylon called Belshazzar who was lavishly entertaining his court with a great banquet at the time the Persian army broke into the city. Unfortunately, there was no other known reference to him, and it was therefore assumed that Belshazzar never existed. Besides, the last king of Babylon was known to be Nabonidus. In 1854 J. E. Taylor, the British Consul in Basra, discovered four identical time capsules from some building works of Nabonidus in which he offers a prayer for himself and 'Belshazzar my firstborn son, the offspring of my heart'. Nabonidus had installed his son Belshazzar in the capital city while he himself went off to war in Arabia. Since 1854 more records of Belshazzar have been discovered.

CYRUS OF PERSIA: THE ORDER THAT WAS NEVER GIVEN?

In 2 Chronicles 36:23 the chronicler records, 'This is what Cyrus king of Persia says: "The LORD, the God of heaven, has given me all the kingdoms of the earth and he has appointed me to build a temple for him at Jerusalem in Judah. Anyone of his people among you—may the LORD his God be with him, and let him go up."'

It was assumed by critics that no pagan king would ever have issued such a decree, since the practice of such kings was to take a conquered people into exile and never to allow them to return. When the Cyrus Cylinder was discovered in Babylon in 1879 that critical judgement on the biblical record was proved to be without foundation. Here, Cyrus recorded his capture of Babylon, but he also tells how he gave permission for many exiled nations to return to their homelands and to take their gods with them and rebuild their cities and temples. Cyrus does not mention the Jews on this cylinder, but since the Jews had no gods to carry around, the Bible records that he gave them permission to rebuild their temple and take with them its ceremonial items that Nebuchadnezzar had plundered.

CAESAR AUGUSTUS OF ROME: A DECREE THAT WAS NEVER ISSUED?

In addition, in the New Testament, the order recorded in Luke 2:1–3 that every man should return to his place of birth to be registered for the purpose of taxation was once considered very unlikely because of the general upheaval and the lack of any known record of this census. However, it is now known that such censuses were a regular feature of Roman rule, and an order issued by the Prefect of Egypt, Gaius Maximus, in the time of Trajan in AD 107 was discovered in 1905 in which every man was commanded to return to his place of origin for the purpose of a census.

10. Authentic prophecy

Whatever our view of the Bible, one of the most remarkable facts is its number of statements and claims that point to a future fulfilment (prophecies).

Sometimes the word 'prophecy' is used to refer to the prophets speaking a message from God. In this sense there may be no future or predictive element involved, but simply a declaration of what God had to say to his people. That is a perfectly correct use of the word, and much of the teaching of the Old Testament prophets was of this nature. Our concern here, however, is to look at some of the evidence of *predictive* teaching: when the prophet declared something that would happen in the future. In many instances these are events that could not have been predicted simply by human foresight.

Prophecy always demanded a verdict from those who heard: either they believed the warning or promise and acted upon it, or they refused to believe and suffered the consequences. Prophecies revealed in the Bible demand a verdict from the reader even today. Either we believe them as yet another evidence of the unique authority and accuracy of the Bible, or else we find some way of discarding the prediction or its fulfilment and accept the consequences. There are no other options.

TELLING THE FUTURE: THE REMARKABLE FACT OF PROPHECY

What is undeniable is the fact that scattered throughout the Old Testament there are hundreds of statements that were fulfilled either in the lifetime of the prophet or later. One writer on this subject has concluded, 'The number of prophecies in the Bible is so large and their distribution so evenly spread through both Testaments and all types of literary forms that the interpreter is alerted to the fact that he or she is dealing with a major component of the Bible.'[41]

To avoid the inevitable conclusion that fulfilled prophecy is yet another example of the Bible as an authentic book there are only two possible approaches:

- We may conclude that predictive prophecy is not possible. However, that is a statement of dogmatic personal belief; reason and evidence point in another direction.

- Or we may conclude that where the prophecy predicts a known event of history, it was written long after the event. In scholarly circles this is known by the Latin term *vaticinium ex eventu*, 'prophecy after the event'. We must believe that no one ever rumbled this constant hoax, and that generations fell for a whole series of monumental frauds and passionately believed them. This is possible, but unlikely.

Of the hundreds of predictive prophecies throughout the Old Testament, many of which have been confirmed by known facts of history, we will select only four examples here.

ISAIAH AND THE BABYLONIANS

Around 700 BC the Assyrian Empire was at the height of its power. Sennacherib their king had invaded Judah, sacked forty-six towns and villages and shut up Hezekiah, the king of Judah, in his capital city, Jerusalem. Throughout the siege, the prophet Isaiah had prophesied that the Assyrians would not so much as fire an arrow into the city (Isa. 37:33–34). Only a miracle from God forced the Assyrian army to

---

41 Walter Kaiser, Jr, *Back Towards the Future* (Eugene, OR: Wipf & Stock, 2003), p. 20.

withdraw (2 Kings 19:35–36). Soon after, the Babylonian king sent envoys to Jerusalem, and in his pride Hezekiah foolishly displayed to them all his great wealth. When they left, the prophet Isaiah warned that in the future the Babylonians would return with an army, and all the treasure of the temple would be carried away to Babylon. Here are his words:

Hear the word of the LORD Almighty: The time will surely come when everything in your palace, and all that your fathers have stored up until this day, will be carried off to Babylon. Nothing will be left, says the LORD. And some of your descendants, your own flesh and blood who will be born to you, will be taken away, and they will become eunuchs in the palace of the king of Babylon (Isa. 39:5–7).

That is precisely what happened just over one hundred years later. Of that there is no question, since both the Babylonian and biblical texts record the sacking and destruction of Jerusalem in 587 BC by the armies of Nebuchadnezzar, king of Babylon. At the time of the prophecy Assyria was the powerful empire, and in 689 BC Babylon was destroyed by the Assyrians. It seemed impossible that Babylon would ever rise again from the ashes of their burnt city. However, in 612 BC the Babylonians had recovered, rebuilt their army and were sufficiently strong to wreak their revenge and destroy Nineveh and end the Assyrian power.

That the prophet Isaiah lived at the time of Hezekiah is beyond reasonable question since his existence is mentioned in the records of the Judaean king at this time. Therefore, the only way to avoid the significance of this as a predictive prophecy is to assume that the prophecy was given by someone pretending to be Isaiah after the event. The problem with this reasoning is twofold: first, we have no evidence for this; and, second, the Jews were taught to be on their guard against false prophets who, if discovered, were to be put to death (Deut. 18:20). Isaiah himself mocked the false prophets who could not reliably foretell anything:

'Present your case,' says the LORD.
    'Set forth your arguments,' says Jacob's King.
'Bring in your idols to tell us
    what is going to happen.
Tell us what the former things were,

so that we may consider them
and know their final outcome.
Or declare to us the things to come,
tell us what the future holds,
so that we may know you are gods.
Do something, whether good or bad,
so that we will be dismayed and filled with fear.
But you are less than nothing
and your works are utterly worthless;
he who chooses you is detestable' (Isa. 41:21–24).

Years later, the biblical prophet Ezekiel, when prophesying of the coming destruction of Jerusalem, could claim with confidence, 'When all this comes true—and it surely will—then they will know that a prophet has been among them' (Ezek. 33:33). It was unthinkable for any Jew to imagine that a prophet would write up his 'prophecy' after the event. The Jews were not that gullible! If he was found out, a false prophet would be stoned to death and his writing would certainly never enter the list of Hebrew Scriptures.

NAHUM AND THE ASSYRIANS

The book of Nahum in the Bible contains a clear prophecy of that final destruction of Nineveh, the capital of the powerful Assyrian Empire. Nineveh was the greatest city of the Ancient Near East, being one and a half times larger than its rival, Babylon, and about twice as large as Rome at its greatest extent. Sennacherib ruled from 705 to 681 BC and turned Nineveh into a capital more glorious than any previously known. He spent lavishly on creating one of the wonders of the ancient world by constructing a new city wall with eighteen gates, temples, roads, bridges, canals and a great palace called 'The Palace without Rival'. Sennacherib filled his new city with plazas, gardens and a large botanical and zoological park next to his palace. It was vast, impressive and impregnable.

Nahum gives us a clue as to when he issued his prophecy by mentioning the overthrow of Thebes in Egypt. In 663 BC the armies of Assyria laid siege to Thebes, and Nahum clearly looked back to this event as one that was in the past. At this moment of Assyria's undisputed power, Nahum looked forward to the destruction of the very city that had destroyed Thebes:

Are you better than Thebes,
  situated on the Nile,
  with water around her? ...
Yet she was taken captive
  and went into exile ...
You too will become drunk;
  you will go into hiding
  and seek refuge from the enemy   (Nahum 3:8, 10–11).

Nahum prophesied after the fall of Thebes in 663 but before the destruction of Nineveh in 612 BC.

Once more we must stress that the Jews were not so gullible that they accepted the retrospective prophecy of an event by a prophet they knew to be still among them and then added his deception to their sacred canon of Scripture.

Therefore, could the author have been writing many years after the event and even after the lifetimes of any who could have witnessed it? This is the argument most favoured by scholars who cannot accept Bible prophecy. However, there are significant problems with this suggestion.

The city was so destroyed and deserted that it slowly disintegrated and, within a short time, disappeared altogether. Nothing was known of Nineveh until it was discovered in 1847 by the archaeologist Austin Henry Layard. No one writing long after the event would have been able to record the accurate details that Nahum includes. Nahum vividly mocked the city with pictures that reflect exactly what we now know of it. The royal lion hunt was illustrated by scores of wall reliefs (Nahum 2:11–13); the amassed gold and silver from the many nations it defeated was unimaginable (2:9–10); and its cruelty was feared by all (3:1). To read Nahum is to read a description by one who must have known the city in its prime; it fits perfectly with what we now know of Nineveh.

Nahum also prophesied how this magnificent and impregnable city would succumb to the Babylonians (2:5–10) and adds the detail that it would be destroyed by fire and water (1:8; 2:6; 3:13, 15) and 'pillaged, plundered, stripped' (2:10). The Babylonian version confirms this, claiming that their coalition partners, the Medes, sacked the city.

The first-century BC Greek historian Diodorus Siculus recorded that, due to heavy rainfall and the rise of the rivers Tigris and Khosr, the floodgates were overrun and a section of the city wall dissolved, enabling the Babylonians and Medes to enter the city. Diodorus Siculus is not regarded as a reliable historian so this may or may not have been the cause of the defeat, but certainly in 1847 Austin Henry Layard discovered the fire-blackened wall reliefs, confirming Nahum's report. Babylonian records include the fall and destruction of Nineveh but, tantalizingly, do not record how it happened.

Also, in confirmation of Nahum 3:13–15, excavation of the city revealed that the defenders had narrowed the width of the northern Adad Gate and the south-western Halzi Gate from seven to two metres in a desperate attempt to make them more defensible. The discovery of the skeletons of guards close to the gates, with evidence of blows to their arms, thrust wounds to their chests and arrows embedded in their bones, is testimony to the savagery of the final assault when it came.

The only way that Nahum could have known such detail of the siege and assault was if he had been with the besieging armies of the Babylonians and Medes and, as a good war correspondent, he had been in every place as the action unfolded! That is an unlikely conjecture. The alternative is a prophecy by revelation from God.

Attempts to deny the prophecy of Nahum's detailed and accurate description of the destruction of Nineveh in 612 BC are more difficult to accept than the possibility of its actually being prophetic.

ISAIAH AND THE PERSIANS
The prophet Isaiah has been the hunting ground of Old Testament critics since the nineteenth century. In brief, their theory is that chapters 1 to 39 may have been given by the prophet himself, but the rest is from a much later time and by a variety of authors/editors; no two critics agree who or when. There are two main reasons for this: first, the latter chapters

are concerned with the rise and fall of Babylon and the rise of Persia, which was well beyond Isaiah's time; and, second the style of the second part of the book, it is claimed, is very different from that of the first part. This latter point is, of course, a purely subjective judgement that by no means all scholars agree with, and the first is simply a refusal to admit the possibility of predictive prophecy.

We may be assured that many excellent scholars of Isaiah have no problem in attributing the whole book to the same prophet.[42]

On the point of predictive prophecy, it is interesting to note that even the section generally attributed to the real prophet contains the prediction that the encircling Assyrian army will not break into Jerusalem (37:33–35) and that Babylon will achieve what the Assyrians failed to do (39:5–7); the precise truth of both prophecies is now a matter of established history.

However, one of the most obviously dismissed prophecies of the Old Testament is found in Isaiah 44–45. After the foolish conceit of Hezekiah in showing the Babylonian ambassadors around his palace and armoury, as recorded in chapter 39, the prophet Isaiah warned that this very nation would be responsible for the destruction of Jerusalem (39:5–7). Indeed it was—twice: once in 597 BC and again ten years later. But Isaiah prophesied that Babylon itself would not last. The exiles taken away by successive armies would be returned to their own land (43:5–6), and the gods of Babylon would not be able to stand against the God of Israel (ch. 47).

In the middle of all these reassurances, Isaiah introduced the name of a future king into his prophecy. Assuring the people that Jerusalem would be rebuilt, he informed them that the instrument of making this possible would be 'Cyrus ... my shepherd' (44:28). More than this, he would 'accomplish all that I please; he will say of Jerusalem, "Let it be rebuilt," and of the temple, "Let its foundation be laid"... I will raise

---

42 The nineteenth-century Hebrew scholar Delitzsch comments, 'All the canonical books of prophecy were written and arranged by the prophets whose names they bear ... The collection of Isaiah's prophecies is thus a complete work most carefully and skilfully arranged.' Keil and Delitzsch, *Commentary on the Old Testament*, vol. 7 (n.d.), pp. 53, 56. So also J. P. Lange, *Commentary on the Holy Scriptures*, vol. 6 (1878; Grand Rapids: Zondervan, 1960); E. J. Young, *The Book of Isaiah* (Grand Rapids: Eerdmans, 1965); J. Alec Motyer, *Isaiah* (Tyndale Old Testament Commentaries; Nottingham: IVP, 2009); and many others.

up Cyrus in my righteousness' (44:28; 45:12). The record of the precise fulfilment of this prophecy is found in 2 Chronicles 36 and Ezra 1, and the discovery of the Cyrus Cylinder in 1879 (see page 83) confirmed the detailed accuracy of all this.

What is startling about this prediction of Isaiah's is the fact that he was prophesying at the time of Hezekiah, around 700 BC, but the final destruction of Jerusalem by Nebuchadnezzar of Babylon was not until 587 BC, and the restoration under the order of Cyrus king of Persia took place after 539 BC, the year in which the Persians defeated the Babylonians. How could Isaiah possibly have provided the name of a Persian king more than a century and a half after his time? And how could he have prophesied the rebuilding of the city and the temple at a time when neither had yet been destroyed?

The answer for critical scholars is simple: he could not. Therefore, as we have seen, they divide the book of Isaiah into at least two parts and assume that this section was not written by Isaiah but was invented well after the events. But why should it be so impossible for God to have revealed not only the circumstances of the return of Israel to Jerusalem, but also the name of the king who would order it? The whole point of these chapters is that God is reminding his people of his love for them in spite of their unfaithfulness and that, unlike the idols and their false prophets, Israel's God alone can be trusted to prophesy the future. Chapter 44 is a mocking assessment of idols and their worshippers.

In order to establish his 'credentials', God, through his prophet, is prepared to make a more precise prediction than was usual by addressing Cyrus directly:

For the sake of Jacob my servant,
　of Israel my chosen,
I summon you by name
　and bestow on you a title of honour,
　though you do not acknowledge me.
I am the LORD, and there is no other;
　apart from me there is no God　　(Isa. 45:4–5).

If this remarkable prophecy was fulfilled, the people would *know* that God was on their side. How, we may ask, would such a claim by pseudo-

Isaiah have encouraged the people if it had been made during (or after) the lifetime of Cyrus? More to the point, why would a recognized scam have entered the collection of Hebrew sacred writings? As one commentator has expressed it, this 'worthless comedy' would make the would-be prophet 'an imposter who blasphemously abused the name of God'.[43] Israel's God would be no better than the idols and their false prophets.

A refusal to believe in predictive prophecy is no evidence that it does not happen.

DANIEL AND THE GREEKS

Critics have a somewhat similar problem in the book of Daniel. Daniel lists, in various ways, the future empires that will affect Israel: Babylon, Medo-Persia, Greece and finally Rome. He contrasts them with the eternal kingdom of God. Then, in chapter 11, Daniel provides an outline of historical events between his own day in the sixth century BC and those of the Syrian ruler Antiochus IV in the second century BC. These prophecies of Daniel have put him into the lion's den yet again because many critics cannot accept that he was able to foretell the rise of a number of great world powers.

The prophecy goes well beyond the time of Daniel, who, amazingly, lived and served under five pagan despots, and touches on the rise of the mighty Alexander the Great. Unlike Cyrus, he is not mentioned by name, but the allusion is clear to all who know their history:

[The LORD] said: 'I am going to tell you what will happen later in the time of wrath, because the vision concerns the appointed time of the end. The two-horned ram that you saw represents the kings of Media and Persia. The shaggy goat is the king of Greece, and the large horn between his eyes is the first king. The four horns that replaced the one that was broken off represent four kingdoms that will emerge from his nation but will not have the same power' (Dan. 8:19–22).

That 'shaggy goat' is Alexander the Great, the Macedonian who boasted that he would conquer the world until the world ran out, and who was commonly depicted at the time with the horn of a ram to express

---

43 Lange, *Commentary on the Holy Scriptures*, vol. 6, p. 15.

his masculinity and to identify him with the gods of Egypt. When he died at the age of thirty-two his empire was divided into four much-weakened kingdoms. Daniel included many more striking details in his prophecies.

Again, critics will assume that the writer was recording events that were past, not future. But once more we may ask how this would have been any sort of encouragement to a people under pressure. The words of a later historian are of little comfort, but the words of a contemporary prophet are.

The book of Daniel is a unit, and there is no historical or linguistic evidence that any part of it was written at any time other than the sixth century BC. The book is carefully constructed, with all the chapters working as a unit to develop the whole, though not all are in exact chronological order. Besides, Daniel reflects the background of the Babylonian and Persian empires that he served in, not the Greek. If Daniel was written after the time of Alexander, why did the author not think of inserting an exact reference to the death of Alexander the Great in 323 BC—especially as he died in Babylon, the city of many of Daniel's activities?

Once more we have to ask a few questions of the critics. Why is it so hard to believe in the predictive element of prophecy? Were the Jews who adopted these books into their sacred writings more ignorant of their recent history than modern scholars? Or were they so naïve that they overlooked the obvious prophetic fraud that was being imposed on them?

PROPHECY FULFILLED IN THE LIFE OF CHRIST

If we think of the Old Testament as a large painting and if we are looking for the theme of this picture, it becomes obvious early in our examination that, though there are many parts to it, it is really a portrait of one person. Many details are so precise that, if we were to meet that person outside the picture, we would surely recognize him. The detailed prophecies and descriptions of the Messiah are often so exact and full that when we read the New Testament it becomes almost impossible not to exclaim, 'This is the Man'—or, as Philip explained to Nathanael, 'We have found the one Moses wrote about in the Law, and about whom the prophets also wrote ...' (John 1:45).

Much of the Old Testament prophecy is a portrait of Christ so that, when he came, only the spiritually blind would miss the connection. Since all the books of the Old Testament were completed and accepted as the Scriptures of the Jews many centuries before Christ was born, the argument that the prophecies were written later in order to fit in with the events cannot be used here.

However, before a critic arrives at the only alternative—that the events were invented in the Gospels to fit the predictions—we must remember that the four Gospels were circulating well before the close of the first century and therefore during the lifetimes of thousands who had witnessed the life and death of Jesus. There is no record of anyone denying the events—with the obvious exception of the story circulated by the Jewish leaders that the disciples had stolen the body of Jesus and invented a resurrection (Matt. 28:12–15).

Even the Jewish Targum, a collection of biblical discussions and wise sayings of the Jewish rabbis in the fourth century AD, attests to the life, miracles, death and resurrection of Jesus; though, as we would expect, they give a very different interpretation: his miracles were magic, his disciples stole his body, and so on (see page 16, 'Authentic Jesus', for more on the first-century extra-biblical evidence of the life of Jesus). However, it is stretching credulity to believe that, if nothing like what is recorded in the Gospel records ever happened, there was no one available to come forward and say so. The apostles claimed to be eyewitnesses, so where is the documentation of those who disputed them?

As far as Jesus and his apostles were concerned, there are many more prophecies in the Old Testament that relate to the life of Christ than we are aware of. Jesus taught his disciples from 'the Law of Moses, the Prophets and the Psalms' about himself (Luke 24:44).

In the examples that follow we will focus only on the *facts* surrounding the birth and life of Christ. The 'Outline of the Old Testament' in Part 3 (page 103) adds many more, but by no means all, of the predictions of the Messiah and his kingdom.

Micah 5:2

Micah was writing around 700 BC and was a contemporary of the prophet Isaiah. His message was to bring hope of a future ruler:

But you, Bethlehem Ephrathah,
   though you are small among the clans of Judah,
out of you will come for me
   one who will be ruler over Israel,
whose origins are from of old,
   from ancient times.
Therefore Israel will be abandoned
   until the time when she who is in labour gives birth
and the rest of his brothers return
   to join the Israelites.
He will stand and shepherd his flock
   in the strength of the LORD,
   in the majesty of the name of the LORD his God.
And they will live securely, for then his greatness
   will reach to the ends of the earth.
   And he will be their peace   (Micah 5:2–5).

This fits perfectly with the birth and purpose of Christ, the Messiah. His birthplace was a marker to identify the Messiah child (Matt. 2:1–6). Until that time Israel would be abandoned to the rule of the Gentiles (through many empires, culminating in the Romans), and the Messiah would gather 'his brothers' (see Matt. 12:48) from the ends of the earth (Mark 16:15) and be their peace (John 14:27).

Ancient Jewish commentators all accepted this passage as a prophecy of their coming Messiah, and this is evident from Matthew 2:4–6, where the Pharisees and scribes turned immediately to this passage in response to Herod's enquiry as to where the Christ (Messiah) was to be born. Even after the birth of Jesus, the Jews still held tenaciously to the belief that their Messiah would be born in Bethlehem, and after the Bar Kokhbar war, in which the Jews again revolted against Rome and were brutally crushed in AD 136, Emperor Hadrian turned all Jews out of Bethlehem so that their prophecy could not be fulfilled.

It was only later that the rabbis switched their interpretation, some deciding that their own Messiah *was* born in Bethlehem just before the destruction of Jerusalem in AD 70 but that, as a punishment for the people's sins, he had been mysteriously taken away from them. In other words, even the Jews did not deny that Bethlehem was to be the birthplace of the Messiah or that Jesus was born in that town. It was only much later that the Jews denied that Jesus was born in Bethlehem, but by then it was far too late to counter the truth that they had admitted for so long.

From a human point of view Jesus had little control over the place of his own birth; no critic can accuse him of having manipulated events to fit with the prophecy. This reference to a child is, of course, picked up in a number of places—not least at Isaiah 7:14 and 9:6, where both the virgin birth and the names and character of the Messiah are revealed.

Zechariah 9:9

Rejoice greatly, O Daughter of Zion!
  Shout, Daughter of Jerusalem!
See, your king comes to you,
  righteous and having salvation,
  gentle and riding on a donkey,
  on a colt, the foal of a donkey.

Zechariah was prophesying around 400 BC and the Jews always considered this to be one of their Messianic passages. This is evident in both the Talmud and Midrashim (early collections of ancient rabbinical teaching). So certain were they that their Messiah would ride on a donkey that the Talmud commented, 'If anyone saw an ass in his dreams, he will see salvation.'[44] This expectation from the prophet's words was only reconsidered by the Jews after the life and death of Jesus.

All four Gospels record the fulfilment (Matt. 21; Mark 11; Luke 19; John 12), and each one links the event with the passage in Zechariah. Was Jesus deliberately fulfilling what he knew to be a Messianic prophecy?

---

44 For the references see Alfred Edersheim, *The Life and Times of Jesus the Messiah*, Vol. 2 (1883; London: Pickering & Inglis, 1959), Appendix 9, p. 736.

Of course he was. He knew the prophecy and was making a powerful statement that he was the Messiah. It was either true or a blasphemous claim—and the latter is exactly how the Jewish authorities saw it.

It is the deliberate fulfilment by Jesus of Old Testament prophecies like this that compel every reader to decide whether Jesus really was who he claimed to be, or whether he was a blasphemous con-man. As C. S. Lewis once commented,

Either this man was, and is, the Son of God, or else a madman or something worse. You can shut him up for a fool, you can spit at him and kill him as a demon or you can fall at his feet and call him Lord and God, but let us not come with any patronizing nonsense about his being a great human teacher. He has not left that open to us. He did not intend to.[45]

Isaiah 53

The book of Isaiah is so filled with Messianic prophecies that commentators have suggested it should be entitled 'The Gospel According to Isaiah'. The most notable prophecy is found in chapter 53.

He was despised and rejected by men,
    a man of sorrows, and familiar with suffering.
Like one from whom men hide their faces
    he was despised, and we esteemed him not ...
But he was pierced for our transgressions,
    he was crushed for our iniquities;
the punishment that brought us peace was upon him,
    and by his wounds we are healed ...
He was oppressed and afflicted,
    yet he did not open his mouth;
he was led like a lamb to the slaughter,
    and as a sheep before her shearers is silent,
    so he did not open his mouth ...
He was assigned a grave with the wicked,
    and with the rich in his death,

---

45 C. S. Lewis, *Mere Christianity* (London: Collins, 1969), p. 52.

though he had done no violence,
    nor was any deceit in his mouth   (Isa. 53:3, 5, 7, 9).

Until the first century AD, when Christianity claimed that this was a prophecy of Jesus who was the promised Messiah, the Jews had always understood this passage in that way also. It is clearly written in the context of an individual. Only after the first century did the Jews begin to reinterpret the passage to avoid its obvious implication. Some applied it to various individuals in the later history of Judaism, but the most common interpretations among them were, and still are, to assume that the suffering servant was either the Jewish nation as a whole or the righteous within the nation who suffer on behalf of the ungodly.

The details are precise: despised and rejected (Matt. 27:22–23), silent before some of his accusers (Luke 23:9), assigned the common grave and yet buried in a rich man's tomb (Matt. 27:57–60).

Since no one, however critical of the Bible, denies that the book of Isaiah was written centuries before Jesus was born—a complete copy of Isaiah was discovered among the Dead Sea Scrolls and dated to around 120 BC—and since the details of Christ's death and burial as recorded in the Gospels have never been seriously challenged, once more we must decide how to account for the remarkable correlation between the prophecy and the fulfilment.

Psalm 22

One of the most significant psalms in the Bible for Messianic prophecy is the one that commences with the cry of Jesus from the cross.

My God, my God, why have you forsaken me?
    Why are you so far from saving me,
    so far from the words of my groaning? ...
All who see me mock me;
    they hurl insults, shaking their heads:
'He trusts in the LORD;
    let the LORD rescue him.
Let him deliver him,
    since he delights in him' ...
I am poured out like water,

and all my bones are out of joint.
My heart has turned to wax;
it has melted away within me.
My strength is dried up like a potsherd,
and my tongue sticks to the roof of my mouth;
you lay me in the dust of death.
Dogs have surrounded me;
a band of evil men has encircled me,
they have pierced my hands and my feet.
I can count all my bones;
people stare and gloat over me.
They divide my garments among them
and cast lots for my clothing ...
All the ends of the earth
will remember and turn to the LORD,
and all the families of the nations
will bow down before him,
for dominion belongs to the LORD
and he rules over the nations ...
Posterity will serve him;
future generations will be told about the LORD.
They will proclaim his righteousness
to a people yet unborn—
for he has done it   (Ps. 22:1, 7–8, 14–18, 27–28, 30–31).

This is a psalm of David and therefore can be dated to nine hundred years before Jesus was born. Even the most critical suggestion admits it was written a few centuries before Jesus' birth. Clearly the writer was expressing something of his own experience, but the theme goes well beyond that; the writer himself must have wondered why he was describing some of the details here. It was quite deliberate on the part of Jesus that he chose this cry as one of his own final utterances on the cross: 'My God, my God, why have you forsaken me?' (Matt. 27:46).

However, there is far more in the psalm than this. It includes the mocking and scorn of the Pharisees and those who passed by (Matt. 27:43); the actual crucifixion itself: 'they have pierced my hands and my feet' (if this is David it was at a time when crucifixion, as we know it, had not become established as a common method of despatching criminals); and the casting of lots for the prisoner's clothes (John 19:24). Added to this we have a vivid picture of someone left for the pitiless burning sun to dry up the tortured body. All this is too closely fulfilled in the crucifixion story to be casually overlooked.

The attempts to avoid a prophetic note in this psalm are varied. Some see it simply as the expression of an individual person and no more; others, that it refers to all the righteous who will suffer; and still others, that it refers to the nation of Israel in its suffering. However, none of this avoids the close application of the details to the death of Jesus. He used the opening verse on the cross, and appears to have followed the last verse of the psalm also, which the Hebrew scholar Delitzsch translates as 'he has finished'—almost the final cry of Jesus, according to John 19:30: 'It is finished.' There is so much in this psalm that details events over which Jesus had no human control as he hung, helpless, on the cross.

So many more
There are many more prophecies of the Messiah that were fulfilled in great detail. Some commentators have calculated that there are more than three hundred prophecies in the Old Testament that refer to Christ, and that twenty-nine of them were fulfilled in the final twenty-four hours of his life.

Accepting some of them as prophecy is a matter of faith and discernment for us, even though it appears to have been obvious to the early Christians. Here are some examples.

The betrayal by Judas was a fulfilment of Psalm 41:9: 'Even my close friend, whom I trusted, he who shared my bread, has lifted up his heel against me.' This is referred to by three of the Gospel writers, although Matthew did not think it was necessary to quote the passage but simply wrote, 'The Son of Man will go just as it is written about him' (Matt. 26:23), leaving it to Luke and John to provide the reference.

Other examples include the massacre of the infants by Herod (Jer. 31:15; cf. Matt. 2:16), the miracles of Jesus (Isa. 35:5–6; cf. Matt. 9:35), the price paid for his betrayal (Zech. 11:12; cf. Matt. 26:15) and his desertion by the disciples (Zech. 13:7; cf. Mark 14:50).

There are many more. While some of them could be argued away, many defy any explanation other than the reality of predictive prophecy; it is otherwise impossible that so many would be fulfilled by chance in the life of one man. We must choose between accepting the fact of prophecy which vindicates who Jesus claimed to be, or rejecting the whole account as a cruel, though disturbingly successful, fraud.

Jesus steered his disciples in the right direction during his final study of the Scriptures with them: 'Everything must be fulfilled that is written about me in the Law of Moses, the Prophets and the Psalms' (Luke 24:44).

Fulfilled prophecy is one of the plainest evidences for the Bible as an authentic book; it resists every attempt to avoid the obvious implication of a God-given revelation.

11. The harmony of Old and New Testaments

The New Testament writers never doubted the unity of the Old Testament, and they saw their own writing as continuing the great story of salvation. When Jesus claimed that he had not come to abolish the Law or the Prophets 'but to fulfil them' (Matt. 5:17), he provided them with their theme.

Far from contradicting the Old Testament or abolishing it, the New Testament writers knew that their Gospels and letters were fulfilling all that God had revealed to the prophets. Paul's explanation of justification by faith in Romans 4 is rooted in the Old Testament account of Abraham, who is used, not as an illustration, but as an example of salvation by faith alone. Paul therefore had no doubt regarding the historical reality of Abraham. Similarly the letter to the Hebrews assumes that everything under the old ceremonies and sacrifices was there to prepare for Christ—a point made forcefully by Paul in Galatians 3:24. Peter was similarly aware that the gospel he and his fellow apostles preached and wrote was that which God first gave to the prophets, who were told, '... they were not serving themselves but you' (1 Peter 1:12).

In this way the New Testament is an extension of the Old and the completion of it. Acts 17:11 records that the Bereans were able to check Paul's teaching simply by referring to their Hebrew Scriptures (our Old Testament). The character of God, the nature of the human race and the reality and consequences of sin, as well as the way of salvation by faith alone through the death and resurrection of Christ, are all consistently taught throughout the unfolding revelation of the Scriptures in both the Old and the New Testaments.

By looking at the plan of God to keep his promise and protect his people, we can see how unique is the narrative that is unfolded in the Bible (see 'God's Big Story' on page 6). There is no other story, and therefore no other book in the world, to compare to the Bible. Far from it being a jumble of ancient legends all thrown together haphazardly, we have a perfect plan that is pressed forward a little further with each book in the library that makes up our Bible. Everything points forward to the Man who was born in Bethlehem of Judaea over two thousand years ago—Jesus Christ.

We are therefore not surprised to find him, at the beginning of his ministry, reading from the prophet Isaiah in the Jewish synagogue in his home town of Nazareth and then declaring, 'Today this scripture is fulfilled in your hearing' (Luke 4:21). Nor are we surprised to find him, immediately before his return to heaven, opening the minds of his disciples to 'understand the Scriptures' so that they could see how the Law of Moses, the Prophets and the Psalms were all fulfilled in him (Luke 24:44–45).

Within this story of God's plan of salvation we have a totally consistent view of the character of God and the spiritual state of the human race since the Fall. Not one statement contradicts another, and never are we presented with a conflicting view of the world or its history. One modern-day critic, as a result of his research into the Bible, declared, 'Now we learn that the Scriptures disagree on the very nature of God'; one is tempted to wonder if he had been reading the wrong book by mistake. That is certainly not what those who have spent a lifetime studying the Bible discover. On the contrary, the harmony of the various Bible books, as they each press forward the plan of God, is remarkable; and it must stand as one of the greatest witnesses to the divine authorship not only of the book itself, but also of the story it relates.

Part 3
An outline of the Old Testament

T he following outline of the Old Testament follows the history chronologically. The 'Preparation for Christ' column indicates some of the main Old Testament texts that prepared for the coming of the Messiah. The fullest (and most exhaustive!) treatment of this subject can be found in the work of Ernst Wilhelm Hengstenberg, *Christology of the Old Testament*. Hengstenberg was a German Lutheran pastor, theologian and tutor in Oriental languages at Basel. He was a prolific author and his three volumes on this subject were published between 1829 and 1835. The page numbers in brackets refer to the English translation published by MacDonald Publishing Company (McLean, VA). A more accessible treatment of this subject is Walter C. Kaiser Jr., *The Messiah in the Old Testament* (Grand Rapids: Zondervan, 1995).

You will notice how the prophecies become more specific and clearer as the time of Christ's birth draws closer—from the general promise to Adam and Eve and the broad sweep of a nation and family (2000 BC) to the specific details of the Messiah (700 BC) and the events of world powers in preparation (500 BC).

The word *Messiah* is a Hebrew word meaning the 'Anointed One'. It is used as an adjective or noun around forty times in the Old Testament (mainly in Samuel and Psalms) and almost always for a king. It is even used of Cyrus of Persia (Isa. 45:1) as the chosen king for the sake of the people of God. In its immediate context Psalm 2:2 probably refers to the chosen king of Israel, but according to Acts 13:33 and Hebrews 1:5; 5:5 it clearly also has a Messianic reference. Some psalms may have the dual reference, but others may be exclusively Messianic because the deity of the Messiah is in focus (e.g. Ps. 45:6–7; cf. Heb. 1:8–9; Ps. 102:25–27; cf. Heb. 1:10–12; Ps. 110:1; cf. Heb. 1:13).

Bible ref.	Approx date	Main content	Preparation for Christ
GENESIS 1 to 11	Before 2000 BC	The Creation. *Adam* and Eve. The Fall. The murder of Abel. God's choice of Seth. The founding of the nations. Babel and the Flood.	The first promise of Christ: 3:15. The first recorded prayer to God: 4:26. The first plan of election: 4:25; 5:3, 29. The promise of God's faithfulness: 9:13–16.
11 to 25	2091 BC	The family of *Abraham*. His call to leave Haran. Abraham in Canaan and Egypt. His separation from Lot. The birth of Ishmael. Destruction of Sodom and Gomorrah. The birth and offering of *Isaac*. Rebekah.	A special people: 12:2; 18:18. A special purpose: 12:3. A special protection: 12:3. A special land: 12:7. A special descendant: 18:7–18, cf. Gal. 3:14, 16; Rom. 4:13.
	2066	Abraham's change of name (17:5).	16:7: The appearance of the 'angel of the LORD' to Hagar. An expression referring to a pre-incarnation appearance of Christ—see also 32:1–24. See also where the Angel is referred to: 12:7; 17:1; 18:17; 21:17; 28:13; 48:16. See later Josh. 5:13–15 and especially Judges. Hengstenberg comments that the early Jews all understood the Angel of the Lord as 'the one mediator between God and the world, the author of all revelation' (p. 1308). Here his deity is also revealed. See also in Zech. 3:1; 12:8; etc.
25 to 26	2006	The birth of Jacob and Esau. The death of Abraham.	The promises renewed to Isaac: 26:4. The choice of Jacob: 25:23.

27 to 35		The story of *Jacob* (*Israel*). The great deceit. His exile and dream at Bethel. Living with Laban, Rachel and Leah	The promise renewed to Jacob: 28:13–15.
36		The descendants of Esau.	
37 to 50	1898	Joseph. Slave, prisoner, Egyptian official. The famine in Egypt. Joseph's sons. Jacob comes to Egypt.	The promise passed on through Judah: 49:8–12; cf. Rev. 5:5.
	1805	*Judah* and the death of Jacob and Joseph.	The Hebrew of 49:10 is literally 'until Shiloh comes', with 'Shiloh' referring to 'rest'. A reference to the Messiah as the man of rest, cf. Isa. 9:5–7 (p. 45).
		Between Genesis 50 and Exodus 1 there are 430 silent years of Israel's slavery in Egypt: Gen. 15:13; Exod. 12:40.	
EXODUS			
1 to 12		'Exodus' means 'the way out'. We are introduced to the oppression of the Hebrews in Egypt and the birth of Moses. Moses is forced into exile and returns to lead the people. The plagues and *Passover*.	The Passover, with its sacrificial lamb and sprinkled blood, pointed to Christ: Exod. 12:1–14; John 1:29; Luke 22:8, 15, 19–20; 1 Cor. 5:7.
13 to 18	1526	*The Exodus* and miracle at the Red Sea. The desert of Shur and the waters of Mara. Elim and the desert of Sin (quails and manna). Rephidim and the battle with the Amalekites.	

	Date	Content	Notes
19 to 31	1446	*Mt Sinai* and the Ten Commandments (three months out of Egypt). God gives Moses plans for living (20–30) and worshipping (24–31).	The purpose of the law was to take charge of us and lead us to Christ: Gal. 3:24; Rom. 4:15; 10:4.
32 to 34		Aaron and the golden calf. Moses prays for the people and the law is renewed.	
35 to 40		The tent of meeting (tabernacle). Gifts offered and the priests and others employed.	
LEVITICUS			The whole book is pointing forward to Christ. The Aaronic priesthood, the Levites, the tabernacle and its implements, and the various sacrifices and ceremonies were all a preparation for Christ, the Messiah. We may therefore refer to 'the gospel according to Leviticus'. The book reveals two great facts: (1) The quality of sacrifice: perfect. (2) The cost of sacrifice: death.
1 to 7		The laws for the tribe of Levi, the priests. The various *sacrifices and offerings*.	
8 to 10		The ordination and ministry of *Aaron and the priests*. Nadab and Abihu	
11 to 22		Regulations for moral, ceremonial and physical cleanness. *Festivals*, rewards and punishments, the law of redemption.	
23 to 27			
NUMBERS		From Sinai to the desert of Paran. Two years and two months out from Egypt.	
1 to 9		A census of the people. Duties of the Levites and the dedication of the tabernacle.	

10 to 12	The people leave Sinai and complain. Aaron and Miriam rebel.	
13 to 14	Spies are sent to Canaan. The people lack faith to go forward.	
15 to 19	Various duties and the rebellion of Korah.	
20 to 21	Water from the rock. The disobedience of Moses and later of the people. The bronze snake.	Paul uses the rock as an analogy of Christ in 1 Cor. 10:4. The snake on the pole was a symbol of Christ on the cross: John 3:14.
22 to 25	Moab and the false prophet, Balaam.	In 24:17–19 the false prophet, Balaam, nevertheless looks on to the Messianic age by reference to the star and sceptre—cf. Gen. 49:10. The ancient Jews saw this as a promise of David and then the Messiah (p. 67).
26 to 30	Another census. Offerings and festivals.	
31 to 36	Destruction of the Midianites. Campsites though Sinai. Levite towns and cities of refuge.	
DEUTERONOMY	The title means 'the second law'. The scene is forty years out of Egypt, in the land of Moab, at the border of the Promised Land.	

Chapters	Date	Summary	Notes
1 to 26		Moses recounts the story of the wanderings from Mt Sinai, forty years before. He includes their rebellion and disobedience, and his own failure. The Ten Commandments are given a second time and Moses urges the people to remain faithful to God. He passes on to them various laws from God.	18:15–19: this 'prophet' was understood by the ancient Jews, the early church and many Reformers to be Messianic (p. 72). See Acts 3:22–23; 7:37; John 1:46; 5:45–47; Luke 24:44. This is the prophet alluded to in John 4:25–26.
27 to 31		Mts Gerizim and Ebal: Blessings for obedience and judgement for disobedience. The covenant renewed.	
32 to 34	1406	Moses' final sermon. The appointment of Joshua as his successor. A song of praise and his blessing on the tribes. The death of Moses.	
JOSHUA 1 to 5		Joshua takes command on the death of Moses. Spies are sent out, the Jordan crossed and preparations made for war.	5:13–15: compare the 'commander of the army of the LORD' with Christ's claim in Matt. 26:53. See also the angel going before Israel in Exod. 23:20–23 (33:15–16); cf. Isa.63:9. The crossing of the sea, the pillar of cloud, the rock from which water flowed, and the manna are pictures of Christ: Deut. 32:18; 1 Cor. 10:1–4; John 6:30–33.

Reference	Content	Date	Notes
6 to 10:28	The central campaign: (1) Jericho and Ai. The sin of Achan. (2) Deceit and rescue of the Gibeonites. (3) The long day at Gibeon.		
10:29–43	The southern campaign.		
11	The northern campaign.		
12 to 19	A list of defeated kings and land still unpossessed. Division of the land among the twelve tribes.		Judah inherits Jerusalem: 15:63.
20 to 22	Cities of refuge and Levite cities.		
23 to 24	Joshua's final charge to the Israelites. The covenant renewed. The death of Joshua.	1356	The people are reminded of the promises to the patriarchs and they pledge their allegiance to the LORD. There is no mention of the Messiah at this point, although he is assumed within the promises to Abraham. Israel's pledge of loyalty is short-lived.

| JUDGES | 1356 to 1050 | The judges, or deliverers, who led Israel for 300 years. There were 15 judges (Eli and Samuel are in 1 Samuel). This is possibly the most tragic book in the Bible. It is the 'dark ages' of the Bible, 2:7,10 explaining the recurring theme of rest, rebellion, retribution, repentance, restoration. 2:11–19 describes the sad cycle of events. Nevertheless, there are some outstanding men and women of faith: Heb. 11:32. | Judges is a record of Israel's unfaithfulness. There is no prophecy of the coming Messiah in the book. The line leading to the Messiah is obscured by sin. However, the 'Angel of the LORD' appears fifteen times and speaks more often here than in any other Old Testament book. The Messiah is active though unrecognized (pp. 80–90). |

CHAPTERS	YEARS	JUDGE	OPPRESSOR	YEARS	EVENTS
3	40	Othniel	Cushan of Aram (Mesopotamia)	8	
	80	Ehud	Eglon of Moab	18	Assassination of Eglon.
		Shamgar	Philistines		Shamgar killed 600 with an ox-goad.
4 to 5	40	Deborah	Jabin of Canaan	20	Assassination of Sisera, Jabin's commander.
6 to 8	40	Gideon	Midianites and Amalekites	7	Destruction of Baal idol. Gideon's fleece and 300 men.
9	3	Abimelech			Abimelech murdered his 70 brothers.
10 to 11	23	Tola			
	22	Jair			
	6	Jephthah	Philistines and Ammonites	18	

	Date		
12		Civil war with Ephraim. 'Shibboleth'.	
	7	Ibzan	
	10	Eglon	
	8	Abdon	
13 to 16	20	Samson Philistines 40	Samson's birth, marriage, wars and death.
17 to 21		A catalogue of anarchy: (1) Idolatry of Micah and the Danites. (2) Immorality of the Benjamites. (3) Civil war between Israel and the Benjamites.	
RUTH		Ruth is set in the period of the Judges, possibly during chapters 17–21. An account of the family of Naomi and her Moabite daughter-in-law, Ruth.	A valuable record of the 'thin red line' of the Messiah preserved during the darkest period of Israel's history. Boaz is a 'kinsman-redeemer' (4:14) and the great-grandfather of King David (4:17–22). Its purpose is to demonstrate that, in the darkest period of Israel's history, God was preserving his chosen line for the coming of Christ.
1 SAMUEL	1070 to 970	The main characters of these two books are *Eli* and *Samuel*, the last of the judges, and *Saul* and *David*, the first of the kings.	There are no direct prophecies of the coming Messiah. However, God is preparing for the line of David, the ancestor of David's greater Son.
1 to 3		The birth and call of Samuel. Eli and his worthless sons.	
4 to 6		The Philistines capture the ark of the covenant. The death of Eli. God punishes the Philistines and they return the ark.	

7	1070	Samuel as judge. His circuit: Bethel, Gilgal, Mizpah, Ramah (7:15–17).	
8 to 11		The defeat of the Philistines at Mizpah. The people ask for a king. Saul is privately anointed by Samuel. Saul's first battle at Jabesh Gilead, resulting in his public coronation.	
12	1050	Samuel's farewell speech.	
13 to 15		The rout of the Philistines at Michmash and the bravery of Jonathan. The sparing of Agag and Saul's rejection by God.	
16 to 27		David is anointed by Samuel. David and Goliath. Saul's envy of David. David the outlaw and friend of Jonathan. During these years David wrote some of his finest psalms.	Compare 16:1 with Ruth 4:21–22. The line of Boaz, from the tribe of Judah, to a simple shepherd boy, to introduce David the king: the great ancestor of the Messiah.
28 to 31		Saul and the necromancer of Endor and Saul's death on the battlefield.	
2 SAMUEL 1 to 5	1010	David is king at Hebron until he captures Jerusalem.	
6 to 7		David is established as king and the ark is brought to Jerusalem. God's special promises to David. David's great prayer.	Although 7:5–16 points immediately to Solomon, the promises go beyond this. Verse 13 looks to the reign of the Messiah. For the 'Name' see Exod. 3:15; 6:3; 23:21.

	God's promises to the king and David's prayer.	Many of David's psalms are 'Messianic'. See introduction above. For example: (1) The Sonship of the Messiah: 2:2. (2) The Suffering Messiah: Ps. 22. (3) The Sovereign Messiah: Ps. 45:6–7; 102:25–27; 110:1. Heb. 1:5–13 quotes from Ps. 2:7; 45:6–7; 102:25–27; 110:1; and 2 Sam. 7:14.
8 to 10	David at war.	
9	David and his kindness to Mephibosheth.	
10 to 12	David's success at war and failure at home. Bathsheba and Uriah. Nathan the prophet. Psalm 51 written at this time.	
13 to 19	Amnon and Tamar, and the exile, rebellion and death of Absalom. Psalm 63 possibly written at this time.	
20 to 21	The rebellion of Sheba and vengeance of the Gibeonites.	
22	A psalm of praise by David when he was delivered from Saul.	
23	David's final prophecy and a list of the members of his bodyguard.	David's final prophecy, with its reference to the Rock and the everlasting covenant, also points forward to Christ: 23:1–7.
24	David counts the people and builds an altar. The death of David is recorded in 1 Kings 2:10–11 and 1 Chr. 29:26–30.	

1 KINGS to 2 CHRONICLES	970–587	This period of just under 400 years covers a major part of Bible history and prophecy. The period from the reign of Solomon to the destruction of Jerusalem and exile of the Jews takes up four history books (1–2 Kings; 1–2 Chronicles), four poetry or wisdom books (Proverbs, Ecclesiastes, Song of Songs, plus some of the Psalms), and fourteen prophecy books (Isaiah to Zephaniah). This is more than half the Old Testament. As the title implies, Kings is the story of the kings of Judah and Israel. Chronicles repeats the history of Kings, often in the same words, but looks more at the spiritual history.	
1 Kings 2 to 11		The reign of Solomon and the building of the temple.	The temple replicated all the ceremonial implements from the tabernacle and therefore continued the preparation for the final sacrifice and priesthood of the Messiah.

| 1 Kings 12 to 2 Kings 25 | | Rehoboam and the division of the kingdom. Rehoboam in the south (Judah) with Jerusalem as capital. Jeroboam in the north (Israel) with Samaria as capital. There were 20 kings in the north until Samaria was destroyed by Assyria in 722. There were 20 kings (discounting the usurper queen Athaliah) in the south until Jerusalem was destroyed by Babylonia in 587. Many early prophets, from Ahijah to Elijah and Elisha, preached chiefly to Israel. Two outstandingly evil kings in the north were Ahab and Jeroboam II, though all the northern kings mixed pagan worship with that of the Lord. Half of the southern kings were good, though Rehoboam, Ahaz, and Manasseh compromised worship. Hezekiah and Josiah saw periods of vigorous spiritual life and reform. | Through the southern kings in Jerusalem God preserves the line of David in preparation for the Messiah. |

PROPHETS	KINGS (An asterisk refers to those who are named in pagan records outside the Bible)				
	Judah (20 kings in Jerusalem)		Israel (20 kings in Samaria)		
	Rehoboam	930–913	Jeroboam I	930–909	
	Abijah	913–911	Nadab	910–909	
	Asa	911–869	Baasha	908–886	
			Elah	886–885	
			Zimri	885	
1 Kings 17 to			Omri*	885–874	
2 Kings 9	Jehoshaphat	870–848	Ahab*	874–853	
The preaching of			Ahaziah	853–852	
Elijah, Elisha,			Joram	852–851	
Obadiah.	Jehoram (Joram)	846–841	Jehu*	841–814	
Micah	Ahaziah	841			
Joel	Athaliah	841–835			
Amos, Jonah	(usurper queen)				
Hosea	Joash*	835–796	Jehoahaz	814–798	
	Amaziah	796–767	Jehoash*	798–782	
Isaiah prophesied	Azariah (Uzziah)	767–740	Jeroboam II	782–753	
from Azariah to the			Zechariah	753–752	
reign of Hezekiah			Shallum	753–752	
			Menahem*	752–742	
			Pekahiah	742–740	
Micah	Jotham	740–732	Pekah*	740–732	
	Ahaz	732–716	Hoshea*	732–722	The fall of Samaria to Assyria in 722.
	Hezekiah*	716–687			
	Manasseh*	687–642			
Jeremiah	Amon	642–640			

	Josiah	640–608	
	Jehoahaz*	609	
	Jehoiakim (Eliakim)	609–597	
	Jehoiachin*	597	
Ezekiel and Daniel	Zedekiah	597–587	The fall of Jerusalem to Babylon in 597 and 587. Many Jews were exiled to Babylon, including Ezekiel, Daniel and his friends.

OBADIAH	c. 848	Obadiah was the first prophet whose ministry is given a Bible book to itself. He prophesied against Edom in the time of Jehoram, king of Judah.	Obadiah reminded Edom that salvation is found only in the God of Judah. Verses 17–21 may have a partial fulfilment in the return from exile in 539, but its ultimate fulfilment is in the kingdom of the Messiah.
JOEL	c. 800	Joel preached to Judah in the time of Joash; through the vivid picture of a locust plague he warned of judgement. But Joel looked beyond, to the coming of the Holy Spirit.	Joel 2:23, 'the autumn rains in righteousness', is considered by most of the older commentators to be translated 'Teacher of righteousness'. No matter how this verse is translated, 2:28–3:21 is clearly looking forward to Pentecost and beyond, to the end of the age. In Acts 2:16–21 Peter saw its fulfilment in the cross and Pentecost. The ancient Jews saw Joel as Messianic (p. 240).

JONAH	c.796	In the time of Amaziah, Jonah was sent to Nineveh, the capital of Assyria.	Jonah was a type of the Messiah: Matt. 12:39–41.
NAHUM	642	150 years after Jonah, Nahum prophesied the destruction of Nineveh, and 30 years later the Babylonians fulfilled the prophecy in 612 BC.	A reminder that, ultimately, all who oppose God and his chosen people will meet with his severe judgement.
AMOS	c.782	Although in the time of Amaziah and Uzziah, Amos preached mainly to Israel in the time of Jeroboam II. A warning against disobedience, illustrated by the surrounding nations and prophetic pictures.	9:11–15 look forward to the age of the Messiah's ultimate kingdom. See Acts 15:16–18.
HOSEA	c.767	A contemporary of Amos in the time of Uzziah, Jotham, Ahaz and Hezekiah. Hosea lived through the fall of Samaria in 722. He speaks on behalf of God against Israel's unfaithfulness, which is illustrated by an unfaithful wife.	3:5: After all the unfaithfulness of Israel and Judah, under the picture of an unfaithful wife, the promise is for the Messiah as 'David their king'.
MICAH		Micah was a contemporary of Hosea and Isaiah.	Micah's prophecies are radiant with the glory of the coming Messiah and the redeemed church. The promises of the 'latter days' are to be taken to signify the time of the Messiah. (1) 4:1–8: The kingdom of God will, in the future, be exalted above all the kingdoms of the world. In these verses is also a beautiful picture of the effect of the gospel when the Messiah comes; cf. Zech. 3:10.

ISAIAH	Both Isaiah and Micah had strong messages of judgement, but offered hope and restoration, both in the immediate future if the nation repented, and in the ultimate promise of the gospel.	(2) 5:1–2: Here 'the reference to the Messiah was, at all times, not the private opinion of a few [Jewish] scholars, but was publicly received and acknowledged with perfect unanimity' (p. 359). cf. John 7:41–42; Matt. 2:6
		Augustine (5th century AD) claimed that, because of his numerous Messianic prophecies, Isaiah deserved the name 'evangelist' rather than 'prophet'. The following are only some of the most pronounced Messianic prophesies in Isaiah; almost all of them were seen as Messianic by Jews—until Christ came, after which they were reinterpreted!
		2:2–5: The ultimate glory of the Messiah's kingdom.
		7:14–16: Immanuel and the virgin birth as a sign.
		9:1–7: A child is born who will reign, cf. Matt. 4:15–16. This whole passage was always treated as Messianic by the ancient Jews (p. 453).
		11–12: The Branch of Jesse; cf. Rom. 15:12; Rev. 5:5; 22:16.
		28:16: The 'cornerstone'; cf. Ps. 118:22; Matt. 21:42–44; Rom. 10:11; 1 Pet. 2:6–7.
		33:17: The future gospel.
		35:5–10: The miracles of Christ; cf. Luke 14:13–21; Matt. 15:31; etc.

		40:1–5: The preparation for the Messiah by John the Baptist; cf. Matt. 3:3.
		42:1–4: The life and ministry of the Messiah; cf. Luke 2:32; Matt. 3:17; 2 Pet. 1:17.
		50:4–11: For the Messiah's obedient life; cf. Matt. 26:67–68; Luke 18:31–32.
		52:13 to 53:12: No passage is used more frequently in the New Testament than this, with eleven quotations and eight allusions. In the Christian church, 'this passage was always considered to be the most distinct and glorious of all Messianic prophecies' (p.620). Until the coming of Christ, almost all Jewish commentators accepted this passage as Messianic (pp.613–618).
		60:19–20: cf. Rev. 21:3–4; 22:2–5.
		61:1–3: The Messiah ushers in the time of the LORD's favour; cf. Lk.4:17–19.
2 KINGS 17	c 732	Hoshea was the last king of Israel. Sargon of Assyria defeated Samaria and thousands were taken into exile, and the land resettled with foreigners.

ZEPHANIAH	c. 640	Zephaniah's preaching encourages the reforms of Josiah of Judah. However, his message is one of foreboding because many of the people are not sincere.	'The Messiah, although not appearing here, stands in the background and forms the invisible centre' (p. 648). 3:9–20 refers to the return from exile in 539, but beyond this it reflects the ultimate kingdom of God.
HABAKKUK	c. 609	In the time of Jehoahaz. Babylon is the powerful empire. After a dialogue with God pleading Judah's cause, the prophet warns Babylon of her eventual downfall.	2:3: The prophet Habakkuk is told that some of his prophecies will be about the end. And that end is briefly but gloriously described in 2:14. 3:16–19: Even in the face of the terrifying Babylonian army, the prophet is confident in God—a timeless message for God's people.
2 KINGS 24		In 609 Assyria fell to Babylon, whose king, Nebuchadnezzar, attacked Jerusalem, put his own puppet king on the throne and carried many into exile.	
JEREMIAH	c. 640	Jeremiah prophesied through the years of the decline of Judah and the two-year siege and destruction of Jerusalem by the Babylonians in 587 BC in the time of Zedekiah. With the capture of Zedekiah, the Hebrew monarchy was at an end. For 50 years the remnant of the people lived almost leaderless in the land. In 592 the governor, Gedaliah, was assassinated and many fled to Egypt to escape reprisals. Jeremiah was taken with them: Jer. 42–43.	3:14–17: Jeremiah looks forward to the Messiah and beyond. 23:1–8: The 'Righteous Branch' who will be called 'The LORD Our Righteousness'. 30–31: 'The whole description in both chapters is Messianic', and 31:31–40 is 'the grand hymn of Israel's deliverance' (pp. 698, 700). These are the promised days of the Spirit. See also 33:14–26; cf. Heb. 10:16–17; John 6:45; 2 Cor. 3:3–6.

EZEKIEL	c. 592	Both Ezekiel and Daniel were young contemporaries of Jeremiah and prophesied during the years of exile in Babylon and later under the Persians. Both looked forward to the age of the gospel and the heavenly kingdom. Ezekiel preached against many nations.	The temple in 40–48 is symbolic of the church and the kingdom of God. 'Its fulfilment under the New Testament is constantly going on, and the future alone will witness its completion' (p. 783). For example see 47:3–4: 'We have here a representation of the Messianic salvation which, though at first comparatively insignificant, will continue to expand with ever increasing fullness and glory' (p. 786). Compare 47:10 with Matt. 4:18–19; and 47:12 with Rev. 22:2. In addition, the following are clear Messianic passages: 17:22–24; 34:23–34.
DANIEL		Daniel 1–6 is history and 7–12 is prophecy. Although it in the Hebrew Scriptures, the book of Daniel is not placed among the prophets. He lived in exile and in high office through six pagan kings. Daniel foretold the kingdoms that would follow from the collapse of the Persian Empire.	2:44 points to the time of the Messiah. 7:13–14: a vision of the 'Son of Man', the Messiah. Jesus frequently described himself like this (e.g. Matt. 8:20 and thirty times in this Gospel). The Jews saw this as Messianic and therefore wrote of the coming Messiah as 'the man of the clouds' (p. 795). 9:25–27: a reference to the final destruction of the temple; cf. Matt. 24:15–16. According to 9:2, Daniel had been studying Jeremiah.
2 CHRONICLES 36		Under Cyrus, the empire of the Medes and Persians defeated the Babylonians.	

EZRA 1–4	c. 539	Cyrus decreed that the exiled nations could return from exile and rebuild their cities and temples. Some Jews returned, but after many problems and much opposition the work halted and the people concentrated on their own homes.	2:59, 62–63 reveals how meticulous was the record keeping of genealogies throughout the history of the Jews. It confirms our trust in the genealogies of Joseph and Mary in Matthew 1 and Luke 3.
HAGGAI		Haggai condemned the people for being more interested in their own comfort than in the temple of God, and he promised a future blessing for the temple.	2:6–9 is a promise of the coming Messiah, before which time the nations will be shaken; cf. Heb. 12:26–28. Calvin explains that 'the condition of the whole world was to be changed by the coming of Christ'. The temple now represents the kingdom of God and the elect will bring the very best to Christ (pp. 944–949).
ZECHARIAH		Zechariah received eight visions which looked forward to the coming of Christ and the age of the gospel.	Zechariah is about little else than Christ; see e.g. 2:10–11; 3:1–10; 6:9–13; 12:10. Compare 9:9 with Matt. 21:5; and 11:12–13 with Matt. 27:9. Each of the visions has a Messianic reference (pp. 965–1182); cf. 3:10 with Mic. 4:4
EZRA 5–10	Sept. 520	The work on the temple recommenced and was completed. Ezra arrived in Jerusalem for the dedication service and effected some necessary reforms. Mixed marriages.	

ESTHER	c.478	A Jewess who was taken as wife for Ahasuerus (Xerxes) of Persia. She learned of a plot to exterminate the Jews everywhere. Esther pleaded with the king, who intervened, and the Jews were saved. The Jews celebrate this in the annual festival of Purim.	The name of God is not mentioned in the book of Esther, but it is all about his purposes in protecting his chosen people and therefore the line of the Messiah.
NEHEMIAH	445	An officer in the court of Artaxerxes I at Susa in Persia, Nehemiah obtained permission to return to Jerusalem and organize the rebuilding of the city walls. Severe opposition was overcome and Ezra again arrived to take part in the dedication of the walls. Nehemiah returned to court and various abuses crept into city life. A furious Nehemiah returned to the city and carried out reforms.	
MALACHI		Possibly Malachi was preaching during Nehemiah's absence at court. He condemned unholy sacrifices, an unholy priesthood and withholding tithes.	Compare 3:1 and 4:5 with Matt. 11:10–15; 16:13–14—the prophecies of John the Baptist as the herald of the Messiah. It is significant that the Messiah, who is promised at the very beginning of Genesis (3:15), is the subject of the last chapter of the Old Testament.

EMPIRE	DATE		
		There are 400 years of silence in Scripture from the close of Malachi to the opening of Matthew. It is known as the 'Intertestamental Period'.	The fourteen books of the Apocrypha—a mixture of history and legend, fact and fantasy—were written during this period. Some of the stories refer to Old Testament events and people, though it also includes the record of the Maccabean wars (167–160 BC). The Apocrypha is never quoted in the New Testament.
The Intertestamental Period			
Persian	539–333	Cyrus defeated the Medes and combined the Medes and Persians into one great empire. In 539 Cyrus conquered Babylon, placed Darius the Mede in charge, and allowed the Jews to return and rebuild their city. His son, Cambyses, pushed the Persian empire from the Nile to India. The biblical record closes around the year 440 with the completion of the city walls of Jerusalem. For two centuries under Persian rule the Jews became a people of the Book (the Torah).	Throughout the entire period between the Old and New Testaments there is no visible sign of the 'thin red line' of the redemption plan. Tribal distinctions were blurred and we can only believe that, unseen and unheralded, God was keeping safe the line of the family of the Messiah until the 'time had fully come' (Gal. 4:4). However, genealogical records were carefully preserved throughout this period, as Matt. 1:12–16 and Luke 3:23–27 reveal. See also Ezra 2:59, 62–63.

	Dates			
Greek	333–323	The temple in Jerusalem was still the centre of worship, but synagogues grew up among the scattered Jewish communities. The high priest became the political as well as religious leader. Jewish territory extended only 12 to 15 miles around the city and the Jews were economically weak.	Alexander the Great defeated the Persians at Issus (northern Syria) in 333. Jerusalem accepted Greek rule without resistance. After the death of Alexander in 323 his empire was carved into a number of rival states: • Macedonia, in northern Greece. • Egypt, the kingdom of the Ptolemies. • The Helespont, under Lysimachus. • Asia Minor and Syria: the Seleucids.	The rapid, though brief, expansion of the Greek empire planted Greek culture across a wide area and Greek became the common language for communication—a vital preparation for the spread of the gospel. Much of Jesus' preaching would have been in Greek, and all the books of the New Testament were written originally in this language of commerce.
Ptolemaic (Egyptian)	323–195		By 311 BC Seleucis I was extending his control. Greek culture (known as Hellenism) was spreading among the Jews. Stadiums were built in the cities and traditional Jews were horrified at the nakedness of the Greek games and the cult of the gods.	Around 250 BC the Old Testament was translated into Greek; it was known as the Septuagint.

| Seleucid (Syrian) | 195–163 | In the reign of Antiochus IV tension flared. In 167 BC hundreds of Hasidim Jews (the 'godly ones') were massacred, the law was destroyed, and the temple and altar were turned over to the cult of Zeus. Pig flesh (abhorrent to the Jews) was offered in the temple and Jews were forced to eat it. The result was the Maccabean wars from 167–160. Judas Maccabeus regained Jerusalem and cleansed the temple and altar. After many brilliant victories, Judas was finally defeated. However, as the Syrian grip declined, the Jews regained their independence, though with factions and bloodshed, until the Romans arrived, and the nationalist cause was lost. | |
| Roman | from 63 BC | In 63 BC Roman troops entered Palestine and the gates of Jerusalem were opened to them. The Jews were granted control of their internal affairs with a Roman governor. Freedom of worship was guaranteed. In 40 BC the Roman Senate appointed Herod 'King of the Jews', and with the aid of Roman troops he gained control in 37 BC. Herod the Great was a renowned builder, a political adventurer and a cruel tyrant. However, he brought national peace and a degree of prosperity. | A relatively stable government throughout a far-flung empire. Good communication by road and sea provided an excellent preparation for the spread of the gospel. |

Part 4
The last week in
the life of Christ

There are different views regarding the details of the last week in Christ's life. The suggestion here for the days of the arrest, trial and crucifixion of Jesus generally follows that of Colin Humphreys in *The Mystery of the Last Supper* (Cambridge: Cambridge University Press, 2003). A summary can be found in Clive Anderson and Brian Edwards, *Evidence for the Bible*, pages 205–207.

Day and Main Events	OT Text	Matthew	Mark	Luke	John
Sunday					
Late in the afternoon at the beginning of Passover week April AD 33.					
The disciples fetch the colt and Christ rides into Jerusalem.	Zech. 9:9	21:1–11	11:1–10	19:28–38	12:12–19
The Pharisees rebuke Christ. His reply and weeping over the city.				19:39–44	
Christ enters the temple, but because it is late he returns to Bethany.			11:11		
Monday					
Early morning. The fig tree cursed.		21:18–19	11:12–14		
The temple cleared and the children's praise.	Isa. 56:7 Jer. 7:11 Ps. 8:2	21:12–16	11:15–19	19:45–46	
Teaching in the temple during the day and spending each night on the Mount of Olives, possibly in Gethsemane.				19:47 21:37–38	
Perhaps it was on Monday that the Greeks asked to speak with Jesus.					12:20–36
The light is with them only for a short time.					12:35–36
The Jews will not believe.	Isa. 6:10; 53:1				12:37–43

Tuesday and Wednesday	OT	Matthew	Mark	Luke
The fig tree withered		21:20–22	11:20–26	
At the temple Jesus is questioned about his authority. His reply is: 'Where was John's authority?'		21:23–27	11:27–33	20:1–8
Three parables concerned with obedience and being ready for his return:				
• The two sons		21:28–32		
• The tenant farmers	Ps. 118:22,23	21:33–46	12:1–12	20:9–19
• The wedding banquet		22:1–14		
Three tests by the Pharisees/Sadducees:				
• Taxes to Caesar		22:15–22	12:13–17	20:20–26
• Marriage and the resurrection	Deut. 25:5–6	22:23–33	12:18–27	20:27–40
• The greatest commandment?		22:34–40	12:28–34	
Teaching the people:				
• About his deity	Ps. 110:1	22:41–46	12:35–37	20:41–44
• Against the scribes	Ps. 118:26	23:1–39	12:38–40	20:45–47
• Seven warnings		23:13–32		
The widow's gift			12:41–44	21:1–4
Towards evening, on Mt of Olives, Jesus' prophecy of the destruction of Jerusalem and teaching of his second coming	Isa. 13:10; 34:4 Dan. 9:27	24:1–51	13:1–37	21:5–36
Three parables illustrating the need to be ready:				
• Ten virgins: preparation		25:1–13		
• Talents: service		25:14–30		
• Sheep and goats: separation		25:31–46		
Two days before the Feast of Unleavened Bread		26:2	14:1–2	
At Bethany, in the home of Simon the leper, Mary anoints Christ		26:6–13	14:3–9	
Judas betrays Jesus		26:14–16	14:10–11	22:1–6

Wednesday evening 1 April AD 33					
The last meal together		26:17-19	14:12-16	22:7-13	
Interrupted by Jesus washing the disciples' feet					13:1-17
Warning of betrayal—Judas leaves	Ps.41:9	26:20-25			13:18-30
The bread and wine		26:26-29	14:17-25	22:14-23	
The disciples argue over who is the greatest				22:24-30	
A command to love one another					13:34-35
A warning to Peter and the disciples	Isa. 53:12; Zech. 13:7	26:31-35	14:27-31	22:31-38	13:36-38
Teaching his disciples at the supper:					
• Christ the only way					14:1-14
• Promise of the Holy Spirit					14:15-31
• Abiding in Christ (the vine)					15:1-17
• Opposition from the world					15:18-16:4
• Work of the Holy Spirit					16:5-16
The disciples believe!					16:29-32
The Lord's great prayer					17:1-26
• For the Father's glory					
• For the disciples' security					
• For the Christians' unity					

	OT	Matthew	Mark	Luke	John
Late Wednesday evening or very early Thursday morning					
In Gethsemane					
Jesus' final prayer and arrest		26:36–56	14:32–51	22:39–53	18:1–12
Early on Thursday his first trial before Annas and Caiaphas		26:57–68	14:53–65	22:54	18:13–14, 19–23
Peter's denial		26:69–75	14:66–72	22:54–62	18:15–18, 25–27
Jesus mocked and beaten. Most likely he was imprisoned overnight in the house of Caiaphas.				22:63–65	
The dream of Pilate's wife this night?		27:19			
During Thursday					
His trial before the Sanhedrin		27:1–2	15:1	22:66–71	
Judas hangs himself	Zech. 11:12–13; (Jer. 32); Ps. 69:25; 109:8	27:3–10			
Christ on trial before Pilate. Barabbas released		27:11–26	15:1–15	23:1–7	18:28–19:16

Event	Old Testament	Matthew	Mark	Luke	John
Early on Friday					
On trial before Herod				23:8-12	
Before Pilate again				23:13-25	
The soldiers mock and beat Christ		27:27-31	15:16-20		
Simon of Cyrene carries Christ's cross		27:32	15:21	23:26	
9 am: Christ is crucified	Ps. 22:18; Isa. 53	27:33-44	15:22-32	23:37-38	19:17-30
The repentant criminal				23:39-43	19:25-27
Darkness from noon to 3 pm	Ps. 22:1	27:45-50	15:33-37	23:44-46	
Jesus died at 3 pm on Friday, 3 April AD 33 (UK time).					
The temple veil is torn		27:51	15:38		
Earthquake. The people at the cross		27:51-56	15:39-41	23:47-49	
Evening: the bodies removed from the cross	Num. 9:12; Ps. 34:20				19:31-37
The burial of Christ	Isa. 53:9	27:57-61	15:42-47	23:50-56	19:38-42
Saturday					
The tomb is sealed and guarded		27:62-66			
Sunday					
The resurrection	Luke 24:27; Ps. 16:8-11	28:1-20	16:1-18	24:1-49	20-21
Forty days after the resurrection					
Christ's ascension into heaven	Ps. 24		16:19-20	24:50-53; Acts 1:6-11	

Part 5
An outline of the
Acts of the Apostles

The formation of the church: Acts 1–12 (AD 33–46)

Luke saw the Acts as the epilogue to his Gospel. For us it is the prologue to world evangelism.

Acts	Date	Location	Events
1:1–11	33	Jerusalem	The final promise and the ascension of Christ.
1:12–26			Judas is replaced by Matthias.
2:1–39			Pentecost and the coming of the Holy Spirit. Peter's first sermon.
2:40–47			Those converted and the life of the early Christian community.
3:1–26			The healing of the lame man and Peter's second sermon.
4:1–22			Peter and John arrested and warned not to preach.
4:23–31			The response of the Christians in prayer.
4:32–37			A further description of the life of the Christian community.
5:1–11			The deceit and punishment of Ananias and Sapphira.
5:12–16			Signs and wonders by the apostles.
5:17–42			Peter and John imprisoned. The miraculous release and a further trial. The advice of Gamaliel.
6:1–7			The appointment of some to serve the community in practical matters.
6:8–7:60			The preaching and martyrdom of Stephen.
8:1–3			The Christians scattered through persecution and Saul set to destroy the church.
8:4–40		Samaria	Philip and Simon the sorcerer and the Ethiopian treasurer.
		Azotus	Philip continues itinerant evangelism.
		Caesarea	
9:1–30		Damascus	The dramatic conversion of Saul and his first evangelism.
		Caesarea	Violent opposition to Saul means that he is sent by the disciples
		Tarsus	back to his home-town of Tarsus via Caesarea.
9:31–43		Lydda	Peter visits the Christians at Lydda and heals Aeneas.
		Joppa	Peter heals Dorcas.

Acts	Date	Location	Events
10:1–48		Caesarea	Peter's vision at Joppa and the conversion of the centurion Cornelius and his household.
11:1–18		Jerusalem	Peter reports to the church in Jerusalem God's work among the Gentiles.
11:19–30	45	Antioch (Syria)	As a result of Stephen's martyrdom, the gospel reaches Antioch. The apostles in Jerusalem send Barnabas to check on the church in Antioch; he goes first to Tarsus to take Saul with him. Agabus prophesies a famine across the Roman empire; the Christians at Antioch plan to send help to the Christians in Judaea. Barnabas and Saul return to Jerusalem.
12:1–19		Jerusalem	James, the brother of John, executed on Herod's orders, and Peter imprisoned. His miraculous escape.
12:19–23	44	Caesarea	Herod's arrogance and self-styled deity end with his excruciating death.
12:24–25		Antioch (Syria)	Saul and Barnabas leave Jerusalem and return to Antioch.

The expansion of the church: Acts 13–18 (AD 46–52)

The first overseas mission: Paul and Barnabas from Antioch AD 46

Acts	Date	Location	Events	Letters written
13:1–3	46	Antioch (Syria)	Paul and Barnabas are sent to Judaea with gifts.	
13:4–12		Seleucia	The sea-port.	
		Salamis	Sea-port and commercial centre.	
		Paphos	On Cyprus, the home of Barnabas (4:36). The Roman governor, Sergius Paulus, converted. The sorcerer Elymas. Saul renamed Paul.	
13:13		Perga	John Mark leaves Paul and Barnabas and returns to Jerusalem.	

Acts	Date	Location	Events	Letters written
13:14-52		Antioch (in Pisidia)	Paul preaches in the synagogue. He recounts the history of the Jews up to David and then applies the gospel.	
14:1-7		Iconium	A chief city in the Roman province of Galatia. A division among the Jews, plot to kill Paul, escape.	
14:8-20		Lystra	A cripple healed. Paul and Barnabas mistaken for gods. Timothy's home-town (16:2). Jewish opposition and Paul stoned.	
14:20-21		Derbe	And the surrounding country. Many disciples added.	
14:22-23		Antioch (in Pisidia)	Returning to home base in Syrian Antioch, appointing elders in each church.	
14:24-25		Perga		
14:26		Attalia		
14:26-28		Antioch	Paul reports to the church and stays 'a long time'.	
15:1-2	48	Jerusalem	Jewish Christians from Jerusalem arrive with a mixture of law and gospel.	Letter to the Galatians?
15:2-29			Council to deal with the false teaching.	Letter of James?
15:30-38		Antioch (in Syria)	The letter from the Jerusalem Council read. Paul and Barnabas sent on a second mission	

The second overseas mission: Paul and Silas from Antioch AD 49–52

Acts	Date	Location	Events	Letters written
15:39-41			Paul and Barnabas part company: Barnabas takes John Mark to Cyprus; Paul takes Silas with him on mission.	
16:1-5		Derbe and Lystra	Revisiting the churches established on the first mission. Timothy joins Paul and Silas.	

16:6–8		Phrygia and Galatia	Paul restrained by the Spirit from entering Asia and Bithynia.	
16:7–10		Troas	Paul's vision to go to Macedonia.	
16:11–12		Samothrace and Neapolis		
16:12–40		Philippi	Conversion of Lydia. When a slave girl is converted, Paul and Silas are arrested and imprisoned. The jail is opened and the jailer and his family are converted.	
17:1–9		Thessalonica	Many converted. A riot in the city. Paul and Silas escape.	
17:10–15		Berea	Silas and Timothy left behind to care for the church.	
17:16–34		Athens	Paul debates in the Areopagus with the philosophers. He refers to their unknown god. A few believe.	
18:1–18	51	Corinth	Paul stays with Aquila and Priscilla. Preaches every Sabbath in the synagogue. Silas and Timothy arrive from Berea. The proconsul Gallio dismisses accusations against Paul. This opposition from the Jews convinces Paul he must now concentrate on reaching the Gentiles (non-Jews).	1 and 2 Thessalonians
18:8		Cenchrea	Paul has his hair cut for a vow.	
18:19–21		Ephesus	Paul debates in the synagogue and promises to return.	
18:22		Caesarea	A brief visit by Paul.	
18:22–23		Antioch	Back home for a short while to report.	
18:24–19:1			Apollos from Alexandria in Ephesus. Aquila and Priscilla, who have remained in the city, mentor him. Apollos then leaves for Corinth, where he powerfully debates with the Jews.	

The third overseas mission: Paul from Antioch AD 53–59

Acts	Date	Location	Events	Letters written
19:1–41	55–56	Ephesus	A slow journey through Galatia and Phrygia brings Paul to Ephesus where he stays for two years. The disciples of John the Baptist.	1 Corinthians
			Paul debates in the synagogue and the lecture hall of Tyrannus and accomplishes 'extraordinary miracles'. The Jewish 'exorcists' fail. Many converts abandon their occult practices and burn their books. A riot instigated by the silversmiths over the goddess Artemis (Diana).	
20:1–2	57	Macedonia	Preaching through the area. Thessalonica?	2 Corinthians
20:2–3		Greece	In Corinth for three months.	Romans
20:3–6		Philippi	Paul and Luke sail from Philippi.	
20:7–12		Troas	Paul preaches at length; Eutychus falls from the window but is healed.	
20:13–16		Assos	All these en route to Jerusalem.	
		Mitylene		
		Kios		
		Samos		
20:17–38		Miletus	Paul calls the elders from Ephesus and encourages them to stand firm in the face of false teachers and persecution. He prepares them for his own death.	
21:1–16	59–62	Cos	The journey to Jerusalem.	

Location	Events			
Rhodes				
Patara				
Tyre	Paul and Luke stay with the disciples for a week. An emotional farewell on the beach.			
Ptolemais	A day with the Christians there.			
Caesarea	Paul and Luke stay with Philip the evangelist.			
	Agabus prophesies Paul's arrest in Jerusalem. Paul's response.			

From Jerusalem to Rome

Acts	Date	Location	Events	Letters written
21:16–26	59	Jerusalem	Paul stays at the home of Mnason. Paul reports to the Christian leaders in the city. They encourage Paul to dispel the rumours that he is opposed to the Mosaic law; he undergoes a purification rite.	
21:27–40			The Jews assume Paul has taken Trophimus, a Gentile, into the temple court; a riot begins and Paul is dragged from the temple. He is rescued by the Romans.	
22:1–29			Paul's speech to the Jewish crowd. Mistakenly flogged by the Romans.	
22:30–23:11			Paul defends himself before the Sanhedrin.	
23:12–22			The plot to assassinate Paul.	

Reference	Place	Description
23:23–35		Paul transferred to Caesarea, the headquarters of Rome in Judaea.
24:1–27		The trial before Felix, the Roman governor.
25:1–12		The trial before the new governor, Festus. Paul appeals to the emperor for justice.
25:13–26:32		The trial before Festus and Herod Agrippa.
27:1–12		The journey to Rome. Under the charge of Julius, the centurion, and accompanied by Aristarchus from Thessalonica.
	Sidon	Julius allows Paul to stay with his friends.
	Myra	Here they changed ships.
	Cnidus	
	Lasea	A sheltered bay called Fair Havens. Paul warns of the loss of the ship and cargo if they proceed further because winter is approaching. The pilot and owner overrule.
27:13–44		The storm and shipwreck.
28:1–10	Malta	The hospitality of the islanders. Paul invited to stay with Publius. Publius' father healed.
28:11–16	Syracuse	They stay here for three days here on the final journey to Rome.
	Rhegium	
	Puteoli	Paul and Luke stay a week with Christians here.
	Forum of Appius	Brethren from Rome come to meet Paul. The Three Taverns.

			Paul writes letters from prison: Ephesians, Colossians, Philemon, Philippians
28:17–28	Rome	Paul's speech to the Jewish leaders in Rome.	
28:30–31		Paul spends two years under house arrest preaching and teaching.	
62–?		After those two years it is thought that Paul was released and continued his mission work, possibly visiting Spain, which he had wanted to do (Rom.15:24).	
		During this time he wrote the 'pastoral letters' — 1 and 2 Timothy and Titus. Paul was subsequently re-arrested and killed on the orders of Nero.	1 and 2 Timothy and Titus.

There is debate around the authorship of Hebrews since no name is attached. However, the earliest tradition (from Clement in AD 95) is that Paul was the author; there is no conclusive reason to dispute this. If it is from Paul, it was most likely written prior to AD 64.

The two letters of Peter were almost certainly written sometime prior to AD 64.

According to Josephus, the first century Jewish historian, James, the author of the New Testament letter and brother of Jesus, was martyred in AD 62. If so, the letter must pre-date this.

Dating of the letter of Jude, another brother of Jesus, is uncertain, although it is likely to have been sometime prior to AD 70.

The three letters from John were most likely written after the death of Paul and Peter, who were almost certainly martyred during the reign of Nero. If John was exiled to Patmos under the emperor Diocletian (AD 81–96), the book of Revelation must have been written sometime after the year 81.

Part 6
A daily Bible
reading programme

Few things are more important for the Christian, or for anyone, than to read regularly the Word of God—all of it: the hard, the tedious and the mysterious, as well as the encouraging and exciting parts. There are many fine commentaries and daily reading notes, but it is essential that we know our Bible, and the only way to achieve this is by reading it through—over and over again.

The following plan ensures that in nineteen months you will have read every word of the Bible once and parts of the New Testament twice. For each day, a longer Old Testament portion is followed by a shorter New Testament reading. The brief introductions are not commentaries but simply set the reading in its context. It is vital that Christians should know the history of their faith and how each book of the Bible fits into the unfolding of God's promise and plans.

The titles of the Psalms are not necessarily part of the inerrant Scriptures, but they do indicate the occasion for some of them. Here, the Psalms are placed according to either their title or where their theme seems most appropriate. Always take note of a psalm's title.

If you are not familiar with the history of the biblical narrative you will find it helpful to follow the outline of the Old Testament (see Part 3, page 103) and the outline of the Acts of the Apostles (see Part 5, page 135) in conjunction with the daily reading.

For your convenience, the daily Bible-reading programme and 'Time with God' (see Part 7, page 176) can be downloaded from the Day One website. Go to www.dayone.co.uk and click on 'Downloads'.

Genesis means 'beginning'. It begins with the account of how God created the universe and life in all its forms. This first book in the Bible introduces us to the human race and its development, marriage, sexuality, sin, salvation and the chosen people, language, government, culture, nations, geography, religion, and much more. There is no such thing as pre-history because there is no history before God's record in Genesis. This is God's revelation of origins.

From the time of Noah and the global flood, our focus shifts to the family and descendants of Abraham and God's promise of a chosen people that will eventually lead to the Saviour, Jesus Christ.

Matthew was a disciple of Christ and his Gospel focuses on Christ as King. His genealogy of Jesus is traced back to Adam through the line of Joseph, who was the legal father of Jesus.

1.	Genesis 1–2		1.	Matthew 1
2.	Psalms 19; 104		2.	Matthew 2:1–18
3.	Genesis 3–4		3.	Matthew 2:19–3:12
4.	Genesis 5–7:5		4.	Matthew 3:13–4:17
5.	Genesis 7:6–8:22		5.	Matthew 4:18–5:12
6.	Genesis 9; Psalm 29		6.	Matthew 5:13–26
7	Genesis 10–11:26		7.	Matthew 5:27–47
8.	Genesis 11:27–13		8.	Matthew 6:1–18
9.	Genesis 14–15		9.	Matthew 6:19–34
10	Genesis 16–17		10.	Matthew 7:1–14
11.	Genesis 18–19		11.	Matthew 7:15–29
12	Genesis 20–21		12.	Matthew 8:1–17
13	Genesis 22–23		13.	Matthew 8:18–34
14.	Genesis 24		14.	Matthew 9:1–17
15	Genesis 25–26		15.	Matthew 9:18–38
16.	Genesis 27–28:9		16.	Matthew 10:1–25
17.	Genesis 28:10–30:24		17.	Matthew 10:26–42
18.	Genesis 30:25–31:35		18.	Matthew 11:1–19
19.	Genesis 31:36–32:21		19.	Matthew 11:20–30
20.	Genesis 32:22–34		20.	Matthew 12:1–21
21.	Genesis 35–36		21.	Matthew 12:22–37
22.	Genesis 37		22.	Matthew 12:38–50
23.	Genesis 38–39		23.	Matthew 13:1–23
24	Genesis 40–41:36		24.	Matthew 13:24–43
25.	Genesis 41:37–42		25.	Matthew 13:44–58

26	Genesis 43–44:13	26.	Matthew 14:1–21
27.	Genesis 44:14–45	27.	Matthew 14:22–36
28.	Genesis 46–47	28.	Matthew 15:1–20
29.	Genesis 48–49:28	29.	Matthew 15:21–39
30.	Genesis 49:29–Exodus 1:22	30.	Matthew 16:1–20

Exodus: The account of Moses' birth, around 1526 BC, prepares for the Israelites' miraculous escape from Egypt, their early journeying through the wilderness, the giving of the law of God, and the establishing of the priesthood and tabernacle. All this is the 'shadow' of the ultimate fulfilment of God's promise in Jesus Christ (Heb. 8:5; 10:1).

31.	Exodus 2–3	31.	Matthew 16:21–28
32.	Exodus 4–5:21	32.	Matthew 17:1–13
33.	Exodus 5:22–7:25	33.	Matthew 17:14–27
34.	Exodus 8–9:12	34.	Matthew 18:1–14
35	Exodus 9:13–10:29	35.	Matthew 18:15–35
36	Exodus 11–12:30	36.	Matthew 19:1–15
37.	Exodus 12:31–13:22	37.	Matthew 19:16–30
38.	Exodus 14–15:18	38.	Matthew 20:1–16
39.	Exodus 15:19–16:36	39.	Matthew 20:17–34
40.	Exodus 17–18	40.	Matthew 21:1–17

Psalm 105 traces the history of Israel from Egypt into the wilderness.

41.	Psalm 105	41.	Matthew 21:18–32
42.	Exodus 19–20	42.	Matthew 21:33–46
43	Exodus 21–22:15	43.	Matthew 22:1–22
44.	Exodus 22:16–23	44.	Matthew 22:23–46
45.	Exodus 24–25:30	45.	Matthew 23:1–24
46.	Exodus 25:31–26:37	46.	Matthew 23:25–39
47.	Exodus 27–28	47.	Matthew 24:1–28
48.	Exodus 29–30:10	48.	Matthew 24:29–41
49.	Exodus 30:11–31:18	49.	Matthew 24:42–51
50.	Exodus 32–33:6	50.	Matthew 25:1–13
51.	Exodus 33:7–34:28	51.	Matthew 25:14–30
52.	Exodus 34:29–36:1	52.	Matthew 25:31–46
53	Exodus 36:2–37:24	53.	Matthew 26:1–16
54.	Exodus 37:25–39:21	54.	Matthew 26:17–35
55.	Exodus 39:22–40:38	55.	Matthew 26:36–56

Leviticus is the book of instructions for the priests from the tribe of Levi and those from the line of Aaron. All the ceremonial details prefigure the once-for-all sacrifice of Christ.	
56. Leviticus 1–3	56. Matthew 26:57–68
57. Leviticus 4–5:13	57. Matthew 26:69–27:10
58. Leviticus 5:14–7:27	58. Matthew 27:11–26
59. Leviticus 7:28–8:36	59. Matthew 27:27–44
60. Leviticus 9–10	60. Matthew 27:45–61
61. Leviticus 11–12	61. Matthew 27:62–28
	Acts is the thrilling narrative of the young church in action from the ascension of Christ to a little beyond the middle of the first century. We will read Acts through twice, and on this first occasion we read it straight through without digressing to read the letters Paul wrote throughout his mission journeys.
62. Leviticus 13	62. Acts 1:1–11
63. Leviticus 14	63. Acts 1:12–26
64. Leviticus 15	64. Acts 2:1–13
65. Leviticus 16	65. Acts 2:14–28
66. Leviticus 17–18	66. Acts 2:29–41
67. Leviticus 19–20	67. Acts 2:42–3:10
68. Leviticus 21–22	68. Acts 3:11–26
69. Leviticus 23	69. Acts 4:1–22
70. Leviticus 24–25:34	70. Acts 4:23–37
71. Leviticus 25:35–26:13	71. Acts 5:1–16
72. Leviticus 26:14–27:34	72. Acts 5:17–28
In addition to giving a detailed census of the people who left Egypt, **Numbers** continues the account of the epic wilderness journey.	
73. Numbers 1	73. Acts 5:29–42
74. Numbers 2–3:26	74. Acts 6
75. Numbers 3:27–4:28	75. Acts 7:1–16
76. Numbers 4:29–5:31	76. Acts 7:17–34
77. Numbers 6–7:35	77. Acts 7:35–53
78. Numbers 7:36–8:4	78. Acts 7:54–8:8
79. Numbers 8:5–9:23	79. Acts 8:9–25
80. Numbers 10–11:15	80. Acts 8:26–40
81. Numbers 11:16–12:16	81. Acts 9:1–19

82.	Numbers 13–14:25	82.	Acts 9:20–31
83.	Numbers 14:26–15:41	83.	Acts 9:32–43
84.	Numbers 16–17	84.	Acts 10:1–23
85.	Numbers 18–19	85.	Acts 10:24–48
86.	Numbers 20–21:20	86.	Acts 11:1–18
87.	Numbers 21:21–22:41	87.	Acts 11:19–30
88.	Numbers 23–24	88.	Acts 12:1–17
89.	Numbers 25–26:51	89.	Acts 12:18–25
90.	Numbers 26:52–28:15	90.	Acts 13:1–12
91.	Numbers 28:16–29:40	91.	Acts 13:13–31
92.	Numbers 30–31	92.	Acts 13:32–52
93.	Numbers 32	93.	Acts 14:1–18
94.	Numbers 33–34:9	94.	Acts 14:19–28
95.	Numbers 34:10–36:13	95.	Acts 15:1–21
Deuteronomy means 'the second law': it revisits and expands on the giving of the law recorded in Exodus. After more details of the wilderness journey we are brought to the death of Moses.			
96.	Deuteronomy 1	96.	Acts 15:22–35
97.	Deuteronomy 2–3:11	97.	Acts 15:36–16:15
98.	Deuteronomy 3:12–4:20	98.	Acts 16:16–40
99.	Deuteronomy 4:21–5:33	99.	Acts 17:1–15
100.	Deuteronomy 6–7	100.	Acts 17:16–34
101.	Deuteronomy 8–9	101.	Acts 18:1–17
102.	Deuteronomy 10–11:21	102.	Acts 18:18–28
103.	Deuteronomy 11:22–12:32	103.	Acts 19:1–20
104.	Deuteronomy 13–14	104.	Acts 19:21–41
105.	Deuteronomy 15–16	105.	Acts 20:1–16
106.	Deuteronomy 17–19	106.	Acts 20:17–38
107.	Deuteronomy 20–22	107.	Acts 21:1–16
108.	Deuteronomy 23–24	108.	Acts 21:17–26
109.	Deuteronomy 25–26	109.	Acts 21:27–39
110.	Deuteronomy 27–28:44	110.	Acts 21:40–22:21
111.	Deuteronomy 28:45–29:29	111.	Acts 22:22–29
112.	Deuteronomy 30–31:29	112.	Acts 22:30–23:11
113.	Deuteronomy 31:30–32:52	113.	Acts 23:12–22
114.	Deuteronomy 33–34	114.	Acts 23:23–35

The first of these **psalms** belongs to Moses himself; the rest are anonymous but are appropriate to this period.	
115. Psalms 90–91	115. Acts 24
116. Psalms 92–94	116. Acts 25:1–12
117. Psalms 95–97	117. Acts 25:13–27
118. Psalms 98–100	118. Acts 26:1–18
Moses' appointed successor, **Joshua**, leads the Israelites across the Jordan and into the Promised Land, and divides the land among the twelve tribes.	
119. Joshua 1–2	119. Acts 26:19–32
120. Joshua 3–4	120. Acts 27:1–12
121. Joshua 5–6	121. Acts 27:13–26
122. Joshua 7–8:29	122. Acts 27:27–44
123. Joshua 8:30–10:15	123. Acts 28
	John was one of the disciples of Christ and the writer of three letters that bear his name as well as the book of Revelation. John does not relate the birth or the parables of Christ, presumably because he knew that Matthew and Luke had adequately covered those areas. He deliberately adds some of the miracles and prayers of Jesus that are not mentioned by the others. Half of John's Gospel is devoted to the last week in the life of Jesus.
124. Joshua 10:16–11:23	124. John 1:1–18
125. Joshua 12–13	125. John 1:19–34
126. Joshua 14–15	126. John 1:35–51
127. Joshua 16–18:10	127. John 2:1–12
128. Joshua 18:11–19:51	128. John 2:13–25
129. Joshua 20–22:9	129. John 3:1–21
130. Joshua 22:10–34	130. John 3:22–36
131. Joshua 23–24	131. John 4:1–26

Joshua died around the year 1356 BC at the age of 110. During the three hundred years that followed, Israel was occasionally led by fifteen '**judges**', including Eli and Samuel. It was a period of virtual anarchy, with the tragic downward spiral of apostasy (when the people abandoned God for the idols around them), oppression (through one of the surrounding tribal nations sent by God in judgement), repentance (by Israel as they cried for help), deliverance (by a judge chosen by God)—and the cycle was repeated over again.	
132. Judges 1–2	132. John 4:27–54
133. Judges 3–4:10	133. John 5:1–18
134. Judges 4:11–5:31	134. John 5:19–29
135. Judges 6–7:8	135. John 5:30–47
136. Judges 7:9–8:35	136. John 6:1–21
137. Judges 9	137. John 6:22–40
138. Judges 10–11	138. John 6:41–71
139. Judges 12–13	139. John 7:1–24
140. Judges 14–15	140. John 7:25–44
141. Judges 16	141. John 7:45–8:11
142. Judges 17–18	142. John 8:12–30
143. Judges 19–20:18	143. John 8:31–47
144. Judges 20:19–21:25	144. John 8:48–59
These two **psalms** review the escape from Egypt, the entry into the Promised Land and the unfaithfulness of Israel to their faithful God.	
145. Psalm 106	145. John 9:1–12
146. Psalm 107	146. John 9:13–25
In the midst of the mayhem and misery of the period of the judges, the story of **Ruth** and Boaz reveals God guarding his chosen line, leading to David and the Messiah, Jesus.	
147. Ruth 1–2	147. John 9:26–41
148. Ruth 3–4	148. John 10:1–21

Samuel is the last of the judges and the account now prepares for the monarchy, when the people demand a king in order to be like the surrounding nations.	
149. 1 Samuel 1–2:11	149. John 10:22–42
150. 1 Samuel 2:12–3:21	150. John 11:1–16
151. 1 Samuel 4–5	151. John 11:17–37
152. 1 Samuel 6–7	152. John 11:38–57
153. 1 Samuel 8–9:21	153. John 12:1–11
154. 1 Samuel 9:22–11:15	154. John 12:12–26
155. 1 Samuel 12–13:15	155. John 12:27–36
156. 1 Samuel 13:16–14:48	156. John 12:37–50
157. 1 Samuel 14:49–15:35	157. John 13:1–20
158. 1 Samuel 16–17	158. John 13:21–30
159. 1 Samuel 18–19	159. John 13:31–14:4
Psalm 59 is from David after Saul had sent men to arrest him at his home. The following **psalms**, interwoven into David's life story, reveal his heart for God at all times. The titles to the psalms indicate the occasions for some of them.	
160. Psalm 59	160. John 14:5–14
161. Psalms 1–5	161. John 14:15–31
162. Psalms 6–10	162. John 15:1–17
163. 1 Samuel 20	163. John 15:18–16:4
164. 1 Samuel 21; Psalms 52; 34; 56	164. John 16:5–15
165. 1 Samuel 22–23:6	165. John 16:16–33
166. Psalms 57; 58; 53	166. John 17:1–12
167. 1 Samuel 23:7–24; Psalms 54; 55	167. John 17:13–26
168. 1 Samuel 25	168. John 18:1–14
169. 1 Samuel 26; Psalm 18	169. John 18:15–27
170. Psalms 138–139	170. John 18:28–40
171. Psalms 140–142	171. John 19:1–16
172. Psalms 143–145	172. John 19:17–27
173. 1 Samuel 27	173. John 19:28–42
174. 1 Samuel 28–29	174. John 20:1–18
175. 1 Samuel 30–31	175. John 20:19–31
176. Psalms 42–44	176. John 21:1–14
177. Psalms 45–47	177. John 21:15–25

The identity of the author of the letter to the **Hebrews** has long been disputed. However, the best and oldest tradition is that it belongs to Paul, and the closing verses imply that it was written from Rome during Paul's house arrest there. It was written primarily to Jewish Christians, encouraging them to appreciate the vast difference between their old way of legal and ceremonial requirements and the freedom of faith in Christ. There are magnificent descriptions of the nature of Christ and his sacrifice.

178. Psalms 48–50	178. Hebrews 1:1–9
179. 2 Samuel 1–2:7	179. Hebrews 1:10–2:4
180. 2 Samuel 2:8–3:21	180. Hebrews 2:5–18
181. 2 Samuel 3:22–5:16	181. Hebrews 3
182. 2 Samuel 5:17–6:23	182. Hebrews 4:1–13
183. Psalms 65–67	183. Hebrews 4:14–5:10
184. Psalm 68	184. Hebrews 5:11–6:12
185. 2 Samuel 7	185. Hebrews 6:13–7:10
186. 2 Samuel 8–10	186. Hebrews 7:11–28
187. Psalms 60–62	187. Hebrews 8
188. 2 Samuel 11–12	188. Hebrews 9:1–10
189. Psalm 51	189. Hebrews 9:11–28
190. 2 Samuel 13	190. Hebrews 10:1–18
191. 2 Samuel 14	191. Hebrews 10:19–39
192. 2 Samuel 15–16:14	192. Hebrews 11:1–12
193. 2 Samuel 16:15–17:29	193. Hebrews 11:13–28
194. Psalms 1–4	194. Hebrews 11:29–12:2
195. Psalms 63–64; 69	195. Hebrews 12:3–17
196. Psalms 70; 71	196. Hebrews 12:18–29
197. 2 Samuel 18–19:8	197. Hebrews 13:1–14
198. 2 Samuel 19:9–20:26	198. Hebrews 13:15–25

	Luke may not have been an eyewitness to all the details of the life of Christ, but he had access to many reliable sources, and he promises a careful and orderly account of the birth, ministry, death and resurrection of Christ. Luke, a doctor by profession, was also the writer of the Acts of the Apostles and a companion of Paul on many of Paul's travels.
199. 2 Samuel 21–23:7	199. Luke 1:1–25
200. 2 Samuel 23:8–24	200. Luke 1:26–45
201. Psalms 11–13	201. Luke 1:46–66
202. Psalms 14–16	202. Luke 1:67–80
203. Psalms 20–22	203. Luke 2:1–20
204. Psalms 23–25	204. Luke 2:21–35
205. Psalms 26–28	205. Luke 2:36–52
206. Psalms 30–31	206. Luke 3:1–20
207. Psalms 32–33	207. Luke 3:21–38
208. Psalms 35–36	208. Luke 4:1–21
209. Psalm 37	209. Luke 4:22–37
210. Psalms 38–39	210. Luke 4:38–5:11
211. Psalms 40–41	211. Luke 5:12–26
Kings: Nearing the end of his life, David prepared Solomon to be his successor, overlooking Adonijah, who was the first in line to the throne.	
212. 1 Kings 1	212. Luke 5:27–39
213. 1 Kings 2	213. Luke 6:1–16
214. 1 Kings 3–4:28	214. Luke 6:17–36
215. 1 Kings 4:29–34; Psalm 72	215. Luke 6:37–49
216. 1 Kings 5–6	216. Luke 7:1–17
217. 1 Kings 7	217. Luke 7:18–34
218. 1 Kings 8:1–53	218. Luke 7:35–50
219. 1 Kings 8:54–9:28	219. Luke 8:1–15
220. 1 Kings 10	220. Luke 8:16–25
221. 1 Kings 11	221. Luke 8: 26–39

Solomon is still known for his outstanding spiritual and moral wisdom, which is reflected in these **proverbs**. The final two chapters come from different and unknown hands, and the queen mother of Lemuel closes with a beautiful description of an exemplary wife.

222. Proverbs 1	222. Luke 8:40–56
223. Proverbs 2–3	223. Luke 9:1–17
224. Proverbs 4–5	224. Luke 9:18–36
225. Proverbs 6–7	225. Luke 9:37–50
226. Proverbs 8–9	226. Luke 9:51–10:12
227. Proverbs 10	227. Luke 10:13–24
228. Proverbs 11	228. Luke 10:25–37
229. Proverbs 12–13:7	229. Luke 10:38–11:13
230. Proverbs 13:8–14:22	230. Luke 11:14–28
231. Proverbs 14:23–15:26	231. Luke 11:29–41
232. Proverbs 15:27–16:33	232. Luke 11:42–54
233. Proverbs 17–18:13	233. Luke 12:1–12
234. Proverbs 18:14–19:29	234. Luke 12:13–34
235. Proverbs 20–21:11	235. Luke 12:35–48
236. Proverbs 21:12–22:16	236. Luke 12:49–59
237. Proverbs 22:17–23:35	237. Luke 13:1–17
238. Proverbs 24–25:10	238. Luke 13:18–35
239. Proverbs 25:11–26	239. Luke 14:1–24
240. Proverbs 27–28:8	240. Luke 14:25–15:10
241. Proverbs 28:9–29:11	241. Luke 15:11–32
242. Proverbs 29:12–30:20	242. Luke 16:1–18
243. Proverbs 30:21–31:31	243. Luke 16:19–31

The traditional view of Solomon as the author of this book, mainly because of 1:1, 12, has been challenged. Some conservative scholars place it at the time of the Persian exile, over four hundred years after Solomon, and by an unknown sage who describes the meaningless of life when we leave God out and who impersonated Solomon only as a literary device. The best translation of the word '**Ecclesiastes**' is simply 'The Preacher'.

244. Ecclesiastes 1–2	244. Luke 17:1–19
245. Ecclesiastes 3–4	245. Luke 17:20–37

246. Ecclesiastes 5–7:18	246. Luke 18:1–17
247. Ecclesiastes 7:19–9:18	247. Luke 18:18–34
248. Ecclesiastes 10–12	248. Luke 18:35–19:10
Song of Songs: This book claims Solomon as the author. It is a beautiful poem of true and pure love, but also an allegory of Christ and his bride, the church.	
249. Song of Songs 1–2	249. Luke 19:11–27
250. Song of Songs 3–5	250. Luke 19:28–48
251. Song of Songs 6–8	251. Luke 20:1–19
1–2 **Kings:** Solomon's final years were a disappointment as he allowed his pagan foreign wives to turn his heart and mind away from God. As a result, the kingdom that had enjoyed so much peace and stability began to fragment, as we saw in 1 Kings 11. The succession of Rehoboam saw the division of the land into ten northern tribes (Israel) based around Samaria and two southern tribes (Judah) centred upon Jerusalem.	
252. 1 Kings 12	252. Luke 20:20–40
253. 1 Kings 13:1–14:20	253. Luke 20:41–21:19
254. 1 Kings 14:21–16:7	254. Luke 21:20–38
255. 1 Kings 16:8–17:24	255. Luke 22:1–23
256. 1 Kings 18	256. Luke 22:24–38
257. 1 Kings 19–20:25	257. Luke 22:39–62
258. 1 Kings 20:26–21:29	258. Luke 22:63–23:12
259. 1 Kings 22	259. Luke 23:13–31
260. 2 Kings 1–2:18	260. Luke 23:32–49
261. 2 Kings 2:19–3:27	261. Luke 23:50–24:12
262. 2 Kings 4	262. Luke 24:13–35
263. 2 Kings 5:1–6:7	263. Luke 24:36–53
	This is our second reading of **Acts**, and this time we will stop off to read the letters of Paul where they fit into the narrative. This will appear a little disjointed but will enable us to appreciate that Paul's letters were written into the living context of active churches.
264. 2 Kings 6:8–7:20	264. Acts 1:1–11

Obadiah is probably the earliest of our 'minor prophets', preaching in the time of Jehoram, king of Judah, around 846 BC. He warns Edom for its cruelty and reminds them that salvation is found only in Judah.	
265. 2 Kings 8:1–24; Obadiah	265. Acts 1:12–26
266. 2 Kings 8:25–9:13	266. Acts 2:1–13
267. 2 Kings 9:14–10:17	267. Acts 2:14–28
268. 2 Kings 10:18–11:21	268. Acts 2:29–41
269. 2 Kings 12–13:9	269. Acts 2:42–3:10
270. 2 Kings 13:10–14:25	270. Acts 3:11–26
Apart from his own account of his eventual preaching at Nineveh, the capital of the powerful and cruel Assyrian empire, **Jonah** is only mentioned in 2 Kings 14:25, which places him at the time of Jeroboam of Israel, sometime after 782 BC.	
271. Jonah 1–2	271. Acts 4:1–22
272. Jonah 3–4	272. Acts 4:23–37
A century and a half after Jonah, **Nahum** warned the mighty Assyrian Empire of their approaching demise. Thebes (in Egypt) has already fallen (3:8–10), so this dates Nahum after 663 BC. His prophecies against Nineveh were fulfilled in detail in 612 BC, when the Babylonians destroyed the great city.	
273. Nahum 1–3	273. Acts 5:1–16
274. 2 Kings 14:26–15:38	274. Acts 5:17–28
275. 2 Kings 16–17	275. Acts 5:29–42
276. 2 Kings 18	276. Acts 6
277. 2 Kings 19	277. Acts 7:1–16
278. 2 Kings 20–21:18	278. Acts 7:17–34
279. 2 Kings 21:19–23:14	279. Acts 7:35–53
280. 2 Kings 23:15–24:7	280. Acts 7:54–8:8
281. 2 Kings 24:8–25:30	281. Acts 8:9–25

The first of these three **psalms** was evidently written when the Jews were led into their Babylonian captivity in 587 BC. The second reflects their return to Jerusalem after the decree of Cyrus in 539 BC.	
282. Psalms 137, 126, 146	282. Acts 8:26–40
Jeremiah was the prophet in Jerusalem from the reign of Josiah to the destruction of Jerusalem in the time of Zedekiah and the subsequent Babylonian exile in 587 BC. His warning of the impending judgement on the city made Jeremiah the most hated man in Judah.	
283. Jeremiah 1–2:13	283. Acts 9:1–19
284. Jeremiah 2:14–37	284. Acts 9:20–31
285. Jeremiah 3	285. Acts 9:32–43
286. Jeremiah 4	286. Acts 10:1–23
287. Jeremiah 5	287. Acts 10:24–48
288. Jeremiah 6	288. Acts 11:1–18
289. Jeremiah 7	289. Acts 11:19–30
290. Jeremiah 8	290. Acts 12:1–18
291. Jeremiah 9	291. Acts 12:19–25
292. Jeremiah 10	292. Acts 13:1–12
293. Jeremiah 11	293. Acts 13:13–31
294. Jeremiah 12	294. Acts 13:32–52
295. Jeremiah 13	295. Acts 14:1–18
296. Jeremiah 14	296. Acts 14:19–28
297. Jeremiah 15	297. Acts 15:1–21
	The Council at Jerusalem was vital for the gospel. Jewish converts arrived from Jerusalem claiming that the Gentiles must conform to aspects of the law given through Moses. It was a message of justification by faith and ceremonial works. **Galatians** may be the earliest letter of Paul on record, written around AD 48 (either just before or after the Council), to the Christians in Galatia who were adopting the heresy of the 'Judaizers'. It contains Paul's personal testimony, a warning against the false gospel, and a reminder of the freedom there is in Christ.

	Apart from the usual cluster of critics, there has never been serious doubt about the authorship of the thirteen letters (not counting Hebrews) that have Paul's name on them. They are all included in the earliest lists of the Christian canon of the New Testament books.
298. Jeremiah 16:1–17:8	298. Galatians 1
299. Jeremiah 17:9–18:17	299. Galatians 2:1–10
300. Jeremiah 18:18–19:15	300. Galatians 2:11–21
301. Jeremiah 20–21	301. Galatians 3:1–14
302. Jeremiah 22	302. Galatians 3:15–29
303. Jeremiah 23:1–24	303. Galatians 4:1–20
304. Jeremiah 23:25–25:14	304. Galatians 4:21–31
305. Jeremiah 25:15–26:9	305. Galatians 5
306. Jeremiah 26:10–27:22	306. Galatians 6
	It is generally accepted that the author of the letter of **James** was one of the brothers of Jesus and the acknowledged wise spokesman in Acts 15:13, and therefore not the apostle who was killed by Herod (Acts 12:2) shortly before Herod's death in AD 44. The Jewish historian Josephus records that James the brother of Jesus was martyred around AD 62. The letter of James, probably sent before the Council at Jerusalem, deals with practical Christian living and reminds the readers that our faith can only be seen by the quality of the life we live.
307. Jeremiah 28–29:14	307. James 1:1–18
308. Jeremiah 29:15–30:11	308. James 1:19–27
309. Jeremiah 30:12–31:14	309. James 2:1–13
310. Jeremiah 31:15–40	310. James 2:14–26
311. Jeremiah 32:1–35	311. James 3
312. Jeremiah 32:36–33:26	312. James 4
313. Jeremiah 34–35	313. James 5
	Paul and his companions embark on their first evangelistic mission across Asia Minor (modern-day Turkey).
314. Jeremiah 36	314. Acts 15:22–35
315. Jeremiah 37–38:13	315. Acts 15:36–16:15

316. Jeremiah 38:14–39:18	316. Acts 16:16 –40
317. Jeremiah 40–41	317. Acts 17:1–15
318. Jeremiah 42–43	318. Acts 17:16–34
319. Jeremiah 44	319. Acts 18:1–17
	During his stay in Corinth, Paul was arraigned before the proconsul Gallio, whom we know was in office in AD 51/52. This fixes the date of Paul's letters to the **Thessalonians**. Timothy arrived with good news of the healthy church there in Macedonia and Paul wrote to commend and encourage them; he also responded to their query about what happens when believers die.
320. Jeremiah 45–46	320. 1 Thessalonians 1–2:12
321. Jeremiah 47–48:20	321. 1 Thessalonians 2:13–20
322. Jeremiah 48:21–47	322. 1 Thessalonians 3
323. Jeremiah 49:1–22	323. 1 Thessalonians 4
324. Jeremiah 49:23–50:7	324. 1 Thessalonians 5
	A few months later, while still in Corinth, Paul wrote again to correct a misunderstanding from his first letter and outlined signs of the end times. There are final instructions to pray and work.
325. Jeremiah 50:8–24	325. 2 Thessalonians 1
326. Jeremiah 50:25–46	326. 2 Thessalonians 2
327. Jeremiah 51:1–23	327. 2 Thessalonians 3
	After a brief return to home base in Antioch, Paul set out on his third mission and arrived in Ephesus, where he spent two years from AD 55 to 57.
328. Jeremiah 51:24–44	328. Acts 18:18–28
329. Jeremiah 51:44–64	329. Acts 19:1–20
330. Jeremiah 52	330. Acts 19:21–41

As the title indicates, this is a **lament** of Jeremiah over the destruction of Jerusalem, something he had been prophesying for many years. However, there is hope for the remnant.

Paul's relationship with the church in Corinth in Greece was never easy. He had written a 'previous letter' to warn them not to associate with immoral people, which was apparently misunderstood (5:9–11). Meanwhile, during his time in Ephesus, Paul heard of moral disorders and disunity within the church and wrote this strong corrective in 1 **Corinthians**—which was also resented as interference. Here he also deals with the subjects of the Lord's Supper, spiritual gifts and the resurrection.

331. Lamentations 1	331. 1 Corinthians 1:1–17
332. Lamentations 2	332. 1 Corinthians 1:18–31
333. Lamentations 3	333. 1 Corinthians 2
334. Lamentations 4–5	334. 1 Corinthians 3

Ezekiel was taken into captivity to Babylon with Jehoiachin in 597 BC and from there warns Jerusalem of its final destruction, which came in 587 BC. He also warns the surrounding nations of their own judgement for mocking Judah. The later chapters are symbolic of the kingdom of God.

335. Ezekiel 1–2	335. 1 Corinthians 4
336. Ezekiel 3–4	336. 1 Corinthians 5
337. Ezekiel 5–6	337. 1 Corinthians 6
338. Ezekiel 7–8	338. 1 Corinthians 7:1–24
339. Ezekiel 9–10	339. 1 Corinthians 7:25–40
340. Ezekiel 11–12:16	340. 1 Corinthians 8
341. Ezekiel 12:17–13	341. 1 Corinthians 9:1–18
342. Ezekiel 14–15	342. 1 Corinthians 9:19–10:13
343. Ezekiel 16:1–34	343. 1 Corinthians 10:14–11:1
344. Ezekiel 16:35–63	344. 1 Corinthians 11:2–16
345. Ezekiel 17–18:9	345. 1 Corinthians 11:17–34
346. Ezekiel 18:10–19:14	346. 1 Corinthians 12:1–13
347. Ezekiel 20:1–29	347. 1 Corinthians 12:14–31
348. Ezekiel 20:30–21:17	348. 1 Corinthians 13
349. Ezekiel 21:18–22:22	349. 1 Corinthians 14:1–12
350. Ezekiel 22:23–23:27	350. 1 Corinthians 14:13–25
351. Ezekiel 23:28–24:14	351. 1 Corinthians 14:26–40
352. Ezekiel 24:15–25:7	352. 1 Corinthians 15:1–19
353. Ezekiel 26:1–27:11	353. 1 Corinthians 15:20–34
354. Ezekiel 27:12–36	354. 1 Corinthians 15:35–58

355. Ezekiel 28	355. 1 Corinthians 16
	Paul made what he described as a 'painful visit' to Corinth (2 Cor. 2:1) and wrote again 'out of great distress and anguish of heart' (2:4). At Troas Paul expected news from Corinth through Titus, but hearing nothing and having 'no peace of mind', he moved back to Thessalonica (in Macedonia), where Titus arrived with good news of the repentance of the church in Corinth. Paul immediately sent off 2 Corinthians expressing his hope to visit them soon; this visit is probably recorded in Acts 20:2–3. Paul travelled from Ephesus through Macedonia (Thessalonica), Greece (Corinth), Troas, and on to Miletus.
356. Ezekiel 29–30:9	356. Acts 20:1–16
357. Ezekiel 30:10–31:18	357. Acts 20:17–38
	2 Corinthians, which, as we have seen, may have been his fourth letter to them, expressed his joy at their change of mind and advised them on, among other issues, how to deal with a repentant member. In this letter Paul established his own apostolic credentials and warned against false apostles. Written from Macedonia around AD 58, this letter expresses Paul's hope to visit them soon for the third time.
358. Ezekiel 32	358. 2 Corinthians 1:1–11
359. Ezekiel 33	359. 2 Corinthians 1:12–2:4
360. Ezekiel 34	360. 2 Corinthians 2:5–17
361. Ezekiel 35–36:21	361. 2 Corinthians 3
362. Ezekiel 36:22–37:28	362. 2 Corinthians 4
363. Ezekiel 38–39:10	363. 2 Corinthians 5
364. Ezekiel 39:11–40:19	364. 2 Corinthians 6–7:1
365. Ezekiel 40:20–49	365. 2 Corinthians 7:2–16
366. Ezekiel 41–42	366. 2 Corinthians 8:1–15
367. Ezekiel 43–44	367. 2 Corinthians 8:16–9:5
368. Ezekiel 45–46	368. 2 Corinthians 9:6–15
369. Ezekiel 47–48	369. 2 Corinthians 10

Daniel was a contemporary of Ezekiel and went into exile at about the same time. The book does not follow a strictly chronological order—chapters 7 and 8 immediately precede chapter 5 chronologically. Daniel held office under at least five pagan despots. Nothing negative is ever written of Daniel in the Bible.	
370. Daniel 1–2:13	370. 2 Corinthians 11:1–15
371. Daniel 2:14–49	371. 2 Corinthians 11:16–33
372. Daniel 3	372. 2 Corinthians 12:1–10
373. Daniel 4	373. 2 Corinthians 12:11–21
374. Daniel 5	374. 2 Corinthians 13
	All the evidence points to the fact that Paul wrote the letter to the church at **Rome** during his three months' stay in Corinth in AD 58 (Acts 20:2–3); it was taken to Rome by Phoebe, a member of the church in Corinth. The church met at the home of Gaius, who we know lived in Corinth; we also know from inscriptions that Erastus was a local government officer in Corinth at this time (Rom. 16:23; see also 2 Tim. 4:20). This is the most valuable and concise book of Christian doctrine in the Bible. It deals with the origin of the human race, sin and its results, justification by faith alone, the new life in Christ, predestination, God's plan for Israel, practical Christian living, and more. It concludes with personal greetings.
375. Daniel 6	375. Romans 1:1–17
376. Daniel 7	376. Romans 1:18–32
377. Daniel 8	377. Romans 2:1–16
378. Daniel 9	378. Romans 2:17–29
379. Daniel 10:1–11:13	379. Romans 3:1–20
380. Daniel 11:14–45	380. Romans 3:21–4:8
381. Daniel 12	381. Romans 4:9–25

Chronicles covers much of the ground we have already read in Kings; sometimes the text is identical and elsewhere it adds new information. It begins with the genealogy from Adam and continues through the patriarchs to David. The narrative starts in chapter 10 with the death of Saul. Chronicles takes us beyond the book of Kings, which ended with the destruction of Jerusalem by Babylon in 587 BC, and continues through to the Persian Empire in 539 BC and the decree of Cyrus allowing the people to return to Jerusalem. This time, we will read the books of the prophets at their appropriate place in the history.

382.	1 Chronicles 1:1–42	382.	Romans 5
383.	1 Chronicles 1:43–2:41	383.	Romans 6
384.	1 Chronicles 2:42–3:24	384.	Romans 7:1–13
385.	1 Chronicles 4	385.	Romans 7:14–8:11
386.	1 Chronicles 5–6:30	386.	Romans 8:12–27
387.	1 Chronicles 6:31–81	387.	Romans 8:28–39
388.	1 Chronicles 7	388.	Romans 9:1–18
389.	1 Chronicles 8–9:21	389.	Romans 9:19–33
390.	1 Chronicles 9:22–10:14	390.	Romans 10
391.	1 Chronicles 11	391.	Romans 11:1–12
392.	1 Chronicles 12	392.	Romans 11:13–24
393.	1 Chronicles 13–15	393.	Romans 11:25–12:2
394.	1 Chronicles 16	394.	Romans 12:3–21
395.	1 Chronicles 17–18	395.	Romans 13
396.	1 Chronicles 19–20	396.	Romans 14
397.	1 Chronicles 21–22:4	397.	Romans 15:1–13
398.	1 Chronicles 22:5–23:32	398.	Romans 15:14–33
399.	1 Chronicles 24–25	399.	Romans 16:1–16
400.	1 Chronicles 26	400.	Romans 16:17–27

	Paul left Macedonia and Greece with his companions, carrying the collection for the Christians in Judaea, and they arrived in Jerusalem in the year AD 59. The rest of the book of Acts deals with Paul's time in Jerusalem, his arrest, trial, appeal to Caesar (which was his legal right as a Roman citizen) and his turbulent journey to Rome, where we leave him under house arrest and awaiting his trial before Emperor Nero.
401. 1 Chronicles 27	401. Acts 21:1–16
402. 1 Chronicles 28–29:9	402. Acts 21:17–26
403. 1 Chronicles 29:10–30	403. Acts 21:27–39
At the death of King David we pause to read a cluster of **psalms**, some of which are from David himself. Those entitled 'A Song of Ascents' were used by the worshippers as they approached the tabernacle and later the temple in Jerusalem. Some, such as Psalm 126, which we have read before, were clearly written when the people returned from Persian exile after the decree of Cyrus in 539 BC.	
404. Psalms 101–103	404. Acts 21:40–22:21
405. Psalms 108–109	405. Acts 22:22–29
406. Psalms 110–112	406. Acts 22:30–23:11
407. Psalms 113–116	407. Acts 23:12–22
408. Psalms 117–118	408. Acts 23:23–35
409. Psalms 119:1–48	409. Acts 24
410. Psalms 119:49–96	410. Acts 25:1–12
411. Psalms 119:97–144	411. Acts 25:13–27
412. Psalms 119:145–176	412. Acts 26:1–18
413. Psalms 120–124	413. Acts 26:19–32
414. Psalms 125–129	414. Acts 27:1–12
415. Psalms 130–134	415. Acts 27:13–26
416. Psalms 135–136	416. Acts 27:27–44
From the reign of Solomon.	
417. 2 Chronicles 1–2:10	417. Acts 28:1–16
418. 2 Chronicles 2:11–4:22	418. Acts 28:17–31

	Ephesians, Colossians, Philemon and Philippians are Paul's letters from his house arrest in Rome. Some have suggested imprisonments in Ephesus and Caesarea, although Rome is the most generally accepted. This letter to the **Ephesians** is one of great encouragement, reminding the Christians that they are chosen and called by God, and loved and prayed for by Paul. He reminds them of their new life and union with Christ and emphasizes the gifts and essential unity in the church. The letter closes with instructions on practical Christian living: holiness, relationships and spiritual warfare.
419. 2 Chronicles 5–6:17	419. Ephesians 1
420. 2 Chronicles 6:18–7:10	420. Ephesians 2
421. 2 Chronicles 7:11–8:18	421. Ephesians 3
422. 2 Chronicles 9	422. Ephesians 4:1–16
423. 2 Chronicles 10–11:17	423. Ephesians 4:17–5:2
424. 2 Chronicles 11:18–14:1	424. Ephesians 5:3–33
425. 2 Chronicles 14:2–15:19	425. Ephesians 6
	The **Colossians** were in danger of being enticed by high-sounding philosophy; Paul reaffirms the true nature of Christ in some of the most descriptive phrases found in the New Testament. Typically of Paul, he closes with the pattern of Christian relationships and final greetings.
426. 2 Chronicles 16–17	426. Colossians 1:1–23
427. 2 Chronicles 18	427. Colossians 1:24–2:15
428. 2 Chronicles 19–20	428. Colossians 2:16–3:17
429. 2 Chronicles 21–22:9	429. Colossians 3:18–4:18
	Apparently the church at Colossae met in the home of Philemon, who was a wealthy Christian. One of his servants, Onesimus, had stolen from him, escaped to Rome, where he found the house Paul was renting, and become a Christian. Paul sends him back, accompanied by Tychicus, with this personal letter addressed to **Philemon**.
430. 2 Chronicles 22:10–23:21	430. Philemon

	Epaphroditus had brought gifts from the church at Philippi to support Paul, but had fallen seriously ill. When he recovered, Paul thought it wise to send him back to his home church as evidence of his return to health. Epaphroditus carried this letter with him. Paul writes to the **Philippians** of the humility and glory of Christ, the need for humility and unity in the church, the danger of false teaching and the need for holiness. He closes with his appreciation for their gifts and his usual final greetings.
431. 2 Chronicles 24	**431. Philippians 1:1–14**
The date of **Joel**'s preaching to Judah is uncertain, and therefore unnecessary. The most likely time is during the reign of Joash around 835 BC. He vividly describes judgement by a massive locust swarm but includes the promise of the coming Holy Spirit, fulfilled at Pentecost (Acts 2:16–21).	
432. Joel 1	**432. Philippians 1:15–30**
433. Joel 2:1–27	**433. Philippians 2:1–18**
434. Joel 2:28–3:21	**434. Philippians 2:19–3:14**
The reign of Amaziah of Judah which began in 796 BC.	
435. 2 Chronicles 25	**435. Philippians 3:15–4:23**
Amos was a contemporary of Isaiah and Hosea during the reigns of Uzziah of Judah and Jeroboam II of Israel, commencing around 780 BC. He warned Syria, on the northern border of Israel, of impending judgement, but directed most of his fire against Israel for their unfaithfulness.	The letters of Paul to Timothy and Titus are the last-recorded messages from Paul written shortly before his own martyrdom. He was now no longer under house arrest, but in prison. **Timothy** was a young worker sent to care for the church in Ephesus; Paul advises him how to establish a spiritual leadership in the church.
436. Amos 1–2	**436. 1 Timothy 1:1–17**
437. Amos 3–4	**437. 1 Timothy 1:18–2:15**
438. Amos 5–6	**438. 1 Timothy 3**
439. Amos 7–9	**439. 1 Timothy 4**

Isaiah preached during the reigns of Azariah (Uzziah), Jotham, Ahaz and Hezekiah. He was resident in Jerusalem at the time of Assyria's devastation of Judah in 701 BC. His prophecies are wide-ranging and include all Judah's neighbouring tribes and nations.	
440. Isaiah 1	440. 1 Timothy 5
441. Isaiah 2	441. 1 Timothy 6
	Here is Paul's final encouragement to **Timothy** to stand firm, together with an urgent request for Timothy to join him in Rome, bringing some personal items of Paul with him.
442. Isaiah 3–4	442. 2 Timothy 1
Our reading returns to the reign of Uzziah (Azariah) and Jotham of Judah.	
443. 2 Chronicles 26; Isaiah 5:1–7	443. 2 Timothy 2
444. Isaiah 5:8–30	444. 2 Timothy 3
445. Isaiah 27–28:15; Isaiah 6	445. 2 Timothy 4
	Like Timothy, **Titus**, who was caring for the church in Crete, is given sound advice by Paul for the leadership and relationships within the church.
446. Isaiah 28:16–27; Isaiah 7	446. Titus 1
Although warning of the impending invasion by Assyria, Isaiah looks beyond to the coming of the Messiah and the fulfilment of the promises of God.	
447. Isaiah 8–9:7	447. Titus 2
448. Isaiah 9:8–10:19	448. Titus 3
	John **Mark**, who failed as a young evangelist with Paul and then matured to become indispensable to the apostle (Acts 15:37–39; 2 Tim. 4:11), is generally accepted as the writer of this Gospel. An early record states that he worked with Peter, who guided the writing of this account of the life of Christ.
449. Isaiah 10:20–11:16	449. Mark 1:1–20
450. Isaiah 12–13	450. Mark 1:21–45
451. Isaiah 14:1–27	451. Mark 2:1–17

452. Isaiah 14:28–16:14	452. Mark 2:18–3:6
453. Isaiah 17–18	453. Mark 3:7–30
454. Isaiah 19	454. Mark 3:31–4:20
Hezekiah was a godly king whose reign enjoyed a spiritual revival. However, in his time Assyria devastated Judaea in the year 701 BC.	
455. 2 Chronicles 29	455. Mark 4:21–41
456. 2 Chronicles 30	456. Mark 5:1–20
457. 2 Chronicles 31–32:8	457. Mark 5:21–43
458. 2 Chronicles 32:9–33:25	458. Mark 6:1–13
We turn to a cluster of **psalms**, some by Asaph, who was David's lead musician and whose psalms were sung alongside David's in the time of Hezekiah (1 Chr. 16:4–5). However, the descendants of Asaph in the time of Hezekiah may be responsible for many of these.	
459. Psalms 73–74	459. Mark 6:14–29
460. Psalms 75–77	460. Mark 6:30–44
461. Psalm 78	461. Mark 6:45–56
462. Psalms 79–81	462. Mark 7:1–23
463. Psalms 82–84	463. Mark 7:24–37
464. Psalms 85–87	464. Mark 8:1–21
465. Psalms 88–89	465. Mark 8:22–9:1
As we saw, Isaiah was the resident prophet in Jerusalem during the reigns of Azariah (Uzziah), Jotham, Ahaz and Hezekiah. His book contains some of the greatest prophecies of the coming Messiah as well as following the narrative from Kings and Chronicles. Isaiah was preaching almost 150 years before Jeremiah, and, whereas the latter warned that the Babylonians would destroy the city, Isaiah reassured the people that Assyria would not so much as fire an arrow upon Jerusalem.	
466. Isaiah 20–21	466. Mark 9:2–13
467. Isaiah 22	467. Mark 9:14–32
468. Isaiah 23–24	468. Mark 9:33–50
469. Isaiah 25–26:11	469. Mark 10:1–16
470. Isaiah 26:12–27:13	470. Mark 10:17–34

471. Isaiah 28	471. Mark 10:35–52
472. Isaiah 29	472. Mark 11:1–19
473. Isaiah 30:1–26	473. Mark 11:20–33
474. Isaiah 30:27–32:8	474. Mark 12:1–17
475. Isaiah 32:9–33:16	475. Mark 12:18–34
476. Isaiah 33:17–34:17	476. Mark 12:35–44
477. Isaiah 35–36	477. Mark 13:1–23
478. Isaiah 37:1–29	478. Mark 13:24–14:11
479. Isaiah 37:30–39:8	479. Mark 14:12–31
480. Isaiah 40	480. Mark 14:32–52
481. Isaiah 41	481. Mark 14:53–72
482. Isaiah 42	482. Mark 15:1–20
483. Isaiah 43	483. Mark 15:21–41
484. Isaiah 44	484. Mark 15:42–16:20
	The last mention of **Peter** in the Acts of the Apostles is in chapter 15. Beyond there we cannot be certain of his movements as the focus is on Paul. This first letter was intended as a circular letter and not addressed to one church in particular. Possibly it was written from Rome, which may be coded as 'Babylon' in 5:13, and very likely before Paul's arrival in the city. It focuses on all that Christ achieved on the cross and prepares Christians scattered across the Roman Empire for the severe persecution that Peter knows is about to fall.
485. Isaiah 45	485. 1 Peter 1:1–12
486. Isaiah 46–47	486. 1 Peter 1:13–25
487. Isaiah 48	487. 1 Peter 2:1–12
488. Isaiah 49–50:9	488. 1 Peter 2:13–25
489. Isaiah 50:10–51:23	489. 1 Peter 3
490. Isaiah 52–53	490. 1 Peter 4
491. Isaiah 54–55	491. 1 Peter 5
	Peter warns against false teachers who are already invading the churches, and presents a clear statement of the uniqueness and authority of Scripture. This second letter closes on the positive theme of the promise of a new heavens and earth.
492. Isaiah 56–57:13	492. 2 Peter 1:1–11

493. Isaiah 57:14–58	493. 2 Peter 1:12–2:3
494. Isaiah 59	494. 2 Peter 2:4–22
495. Isaiah 60	495. 2 Peter 3
	Jude was a brother of our Lord and of the James who authored a letter and spoke persuasively at the Council in Jerusalem in Acts 15:13. Jude's short letter contains some of the strongest language against false teachers whose attacks against the person of Christ led to immoral behaviour. This is an indication that it was written later in the first century, when the heretical views and immoral practices of the Gnostics, who confused the simplicity of the historic gospel with strange ideas of inner light and secret knowledge, were gaining ground in many areas.
496. Isaiah 61–62	496. Jude 1–13
497. Isaiah 63	497. Jude 14–25
	The author of these three letters is almost certainly the disciple of Christ, the writer of the Gospel of John and of the final book of Revelation. Like Jude, **John** is clearly combatting early heresies of the Gnostics and those who denied the full deity and the real humanity of Christ, claiming that Jesus only 'seemed' to be God and man (known as Docetism).
498. Isaiah 64–65:16	498. 1 John 1
499. Isaiah 65:17–66:24	499. 1 John 2:1–14
Hosea was a contemporary of Isaiah and Amos. Like Amos, Hosea preached to Israel. He began preaching around 767 BC and continued through the reigns of Azariah (Uzziah), Jotham, Ahaz and Hezekiah of Judah and during the reign of Jeroboam II of Israel. The behaviour of his own promiscuous wife is seen as a tragic picture of Israel's unfaithfulness to their covenant God. Hosea warns of the final judgement on Israel which came in the year 722 BC with the Assyrian conquest.	

500. Hosea 1–2	500. 1 John 2:15–29
501. Hosea 3–4	501. 1 John 3
502. Hosea 5–6	502. 1 John 4
503. Hosea 7–8	503. 1 John 5
	It is a matter of debate whether the 'chosen lady' is a local church or some particular Christian lady. However, the value of this second letter does not depend on this identification. The themes are love, obedience, vigilance for the truth and resisting error.
504. Hosea 9–10	504. 2 John
	We cannot be certain who Gaius was, but this third letter is a warm commendation by the ageing apostle John and a serious warning against Diotrephes, who is spoiling the harmony of the fellowship.
505. Hosea 11–12	505. 3 John
	John's **revelation**, received while in exile on the isle of Patmos by order of the Emperor Diocletian, begins with a description of the risen and ascended Christ and letters addressed to seven churches across Asia Minor (modern-day Turkey). Then follows a vibrant declaration of the glory of Christ and his ultimate triumph over Satan and all the forces of evil. This is presented in a series of striking and vivid pictures. They repeat the same themes: the warfare of Christ and his church with evil in every form, the ultimate judgement of the devil and his followers, and the triumph of the church and its Saviour. Don't worry about the detail—enjoy the big picture. The history of the human race began in a garden with the tree of the knowledge of good and evil, and it closes in a garden in the new earth with the tree of life in the centre.
506. Hosea 13–14	506. Revelation 1

Micah was a contemporary of Hosea. His prophecy is radiant with the glory of the coming Messiah and redeemed church. The promises of the 'latter days' are to be taken as the time of the Messiah and not literal Israel.	
507. Micah 1–2:5	507. Revelation 2:1–11
508. Micah 2:6–3:12	508. Revelation 2:12–29
509. Micah 4	509. Revelation 3:1–13
510. Micah 5–6:8	510. Revelation 3:14–22
511. Micah 6:9–7:20	511. Revelation 4
The reign of the worst king of Judah, Manasseh, up to the destruction of Jerusalem and the temple by the Babylonian army of Nebuchadnezzar in 587 BC. Chronicles closes with a brief mention of the rise of the Persians to power when they captured Babylon in 539 BC.	
512. 2 Chronicles 33	512. Revelation 5
513. 2 Chronicles 34	513. Revelation 6
514. 2 Chronicles 35	514. Revelation 7
515. 2 Chronicles 36	515. Revelation 8
In spite of temporary reformation under the good King Josiah (640–609 BC), **Zephaniah**'s prophecy is one of foreboding because the people are not sincere.	
516. Zephaniah 1–2:12	516. Revelation 9
517. Zephaniah 2:13–3:20	517. Revelation 10
The prophet **Habakkuk** speaks of the rise of Babylon as something unimagined (1:5–11), which would place him in the time of Josiah before Babylon's defeat of Assyria (Nineveh) in 612 BC. After a dialogue with God, the prophet warns Babylon of her own eventual downfall.	
518. Habakkuk 1	518. Revelation 11
519 Habakkuk 2	519. Revelation 12
520 Habbakuk 3	520. Revelation 13
Ezra was a priest sent to Jerusalem in the time of Artaxerxes. He records the people who returned to Jerusalem after the decree of Cyrus in 539 BC.	

521. Ezra 1–2	521. Revelation 14
522. Ezra 3–4	522. Revelation 15
523. Ezra 5:1–6:12	523. Revelation 16
524. Ezra 6:13–7:28	524. Revelation 17
525. Ezra 8	525. Revelation 18:1–10
526. Ezra 9–10	526. Revelation 18:11–24
By September 520 BC the Jews had returned from exile and after a promising start to rebuild the temple they gave up in preference for their own houses. **Haggai** urged them back to work.	
527. Haggai 1–2	527. Revelation 19:1–10
Zechariah was a contemporary of Haggai. Eight visions are followed by promises of the coming Messiah and the triumph of his church.	
528. Zechariah 1–3	528. Revelation 19:11–21
529. Zechariah 4–7	529. Revelation 20
530. Zechariah 8–9	530. Revelation 21:1–14
531. Zechariah 10–12	531. Revelation 21:15–27
532. Zechariah 13–14	532. Revelation 22
Nehemiah, the cupbearer to the Persian King Artaxerxes, the son of Xerxes, became governor of Judaea at a crucial time of opposition to the rebuilding of the temple and the city walls.	This is our second reading of **Mark's Gospel.**
533. Nehemiah 1–2	533. Mark 1:1–20
534. Nehemiah 3	534. Mark 1:21–45
535. Nehemiah 4–5	535. Mark 2:1–17
536. Nehemiah 6–7	536. Mark 2:18–3:6
537. Nehemiah 8–9:5	537. Mark 3:7–30
538. Nehemiah 9:5–38	538. Mark 3:31–4:20
539. Nehemiah 10	539. Mark 4:21–41
540. Nehemiah 11–12:26	540. Mark 5:1–20
541. Nehemiah 12:27–13:31	541. Mark 5:21–43
Esther is the heroic account of one woman saving the Jewish people from genocide. Although God is never mentioned in this book, his providence is everywhere in focus. Esther was queen to Xerxes and therefore strictly her story precedes that of Nehemiah.	

542. Esther 1–2	542. Mark 6:1–13
543. Esther 3–4	543. Mark 6:14–29
544. Esther 5–7	544. Mark 6:30–44
545. Esther 8–10	545. Mark 6:45–56
Sometime after 423 BC and during the time of Nehemiah **Malachi** reminded the Jews how they were despising God's name and robbing him. He foretold the coming Elijah (John the Baptist) as the herald for the Messiah.	
546. Malachi 1–2	546. Mark 7:1–23
547. Malachi 3–4	547. Mark 7:24–37
Malachi closes the Old Testament around 400 BC. The years that follow are filled with the Persians who are defeated by the Greeks under Alexander the Great in 333 BC. The Egyptian Ptolemies were followed by the Syrian (Seleucid) dynasties and finally the Romans, whose legions first entered Palestine in 63 BC.	
The date of **Job** is unknown. It appears to be set in the age of the patriarchs, though its final written form may date to the time of Solomon. With good reason it is widely acknowledged as possibly the finest religious poem ever written. However, it is much more than this because it records the experience of a real man. The narrative faces up to the issue of suffering and both the wise and foolish responses to it. The sovereignty of God is at the heart of the whole debate.	
548. Job 1–2	548. Mark 8:1–30
549. Job 3–4	549. Mark 8:31–9:13
550. Job 5–6	550. Mark 9:14–32
551. Job 7–8	551. Mark 9:33–50
552. Job 9–10	552. Mark 10:1–16
553. Job 11–12	553. Mark 10:17–34
554. Job 13–14	554. Mark 10:35–52
555. Job 15–17	555. Mark 11:1–19
556. Job 18–19	556. Mark 11:20–33

557. Job 20–21	557. Mark 12:1–17
558 Job 22–23	558. Mark 12:18–34
559. Job 24–26	559. Mark 12:35–44
560. Job 27–28	560. Mark 13:1–23
561. Job 29–30	561. Mark 12:24–14:11
562. Job 31	562. Mark 14:12–31
563. Job 32–33	563. Mark 14:32–52
564. Job 34–35	564. Mark 14:53–72
565. Job 36–37	565. Mark 15:1–20
566. Job 38–39	566. Mark 15:21–41
567. Job 40–42	567. Mark 15:42–16:20

Part 7
A daily Time with God

Every morning lean your arms awhile
upon the windowsill of heaven
and gaze upon the Lord.
Then with the vision in your heart,
turn strong to meet your day.

The seventeenth-century Anglican minister Thomas Blake captured in this verse all that, a hundred years later, the American Congregational minister Austin Phelps referred to as 'The Still Hour' and which, a further hundred years on, was known by evangelical Christians as the 'Quiet Time'.

By whatever name it is known, the daily 'Time with God' has been lost in the busyness of the twenty-first century. In many Christian homes, husbands and wives do not pray together and children rarely hear their Christian parents pray at all. If prayers are offered, it is only occasionally and with as little time as we can manage to spare.

The rush of modern life is only one reason for the loss of what used to be an essential feature for every Christian home. We have lost an appetite for prayer because it is no longer seen as the privilege it really is: when a forgiven sinner can boldly approach the immediate presence of the Sovereign God of the universe and call him 'Father'. His ever-listening ear is always open for the voice of his children.

We have also lost confidence in prayer. So many of our prayers are seemingly unanswered. We do not get what we want or expect, so we give up. We agree with the importance of prayer, but leave it to others. Ours did not work, so why waste time?

There is another reason for our abandonment of 'Time with God'. We have so many things for which we should pray that we never quite get started. We may have tried schemes without number, but they all come to nothing sooner or later.

Planned praying is rejected as unspiritual by some Christians, so they are content either not to pray at all or to enter the shallows of prayers that wander around until the mind drifts away.

If the essentials for a healthy Christian life—time with God's Word and time with God himself—are not to be lost altogether, we must reassess their importance in our life and make time for them. But we must do more than make time. We must make both our reading and our praying meaningful.

What follows here is only a guide to keep us focused each day. It will ensure that we do not rush into prayer and badger God with a long list of requests before we have settled our minds on the God we are approaching. An adoring, thankful and repentant heart is what God desires from his people before they come with supplication and intercession.

We must each turn the guide here into our own 'Time with God'. The suggested headings need to be filled out with our personal items for thanksgiving and intercession. There are reliable Christian missions that provide daily prayer guides for persecuted Christians. We cannot pray for everything and everyone each day, but over the course of a week we can bring before God many of those people and concerns that we have often promised to pray for.

The Scripture verses are intended to root our prayers in the Word of God. And there can be no more persuasive prayers with God than those that are based upon his promise and pattern. Some of the deepest and strongest prayers ever written come from the hand of the apostle Paul, so we have taken one of these each day and turned it to our own use.

Our 'Time with God' and his Word is intended to be an enjoyable privilege. Let's make it so.

Sunday

ADORATION

For God in creation

'Who has measured the waters in the hollow of his hand, or with the breadth of his hand marked off the heavens? Who has held the dust of the earth in a basket, or weighed the mountains on the scales and the hills in a balance? Who has understood the mind of the LORD, or instructed him as his counsellor? Whom did the LORD consult to enlighten him, and who taught him the right way? Who was it that taught him knowledge or showed him the path of understanding?' Isa. 40:12–14).

CONFESSION

'Jesus replied: " 'Love the Lord your God with all your heart and with all your soul and with all your mind.' This is the first and greatest commandment. And the second is like it: 'Love your neighbour as yourself' " ' (Matt. 22:37–39).

THANKSGIVING

For the Lord's day

'By the seventh day God had finished the work he had been doing; so on the seventh day he rested from all his work. And God blessed the seventh day and made it holy, because on it he rested from all the work of creating that he had done' Gen. 2:2–3).

For our home and family

'As for me and my household, we will serve the Lord' (Josh. 24:15).

For preaching and Christian fellowship

'I always pray with joy because of your partnership in the gospel from the first day until now' (Phil. 1:4–5).

SUPPLICATION

For ourselves, our family and our church

We pray that out of your glorious riches you will strengthen us with power through your Spirit in our inner being, so that Christ may dwell in our hearts through faith. And we pray that, being rooted and established in love, we may have power, together with all the saints, to grasp how wide and long and high and deep is the love of Christ, and to know this love that surpasses knowledge—that we may be filled to the measure of all the fullness of God (based on Eph. 3:16–19).

For preachers to preach with attractive and Holy Spirit power

'My message and my preaching were not with wise and persuasive words, but with a demonstration of the Spirit's power, so that your faith might not rest on men's wisdom, but on God's power' (1 Cor. 2:4–5).

For revival

'Although our sins testify against us, O LORD, do something for the sake of your name. For our backsliding is great; we have sinned against you ... O Lord, we acknowledge our wickedness and the guilt of our fathers; we have indeed sinned against you. For the sake of your name do not despise us; do not dishonour your glorious throne. Remember your covenant with us and do not break it' (Jer. 14:7, 20–21).

INTERCESSION FOR OTHERS

For persecuted Christians

'Remember those in prison as if you were their fellow-prisoners, and those who are ill-treated as if you yourselves were suffering' (Heb. 13:3).

For our missionary friends and missions

'Pray for us that the message of the Lord may spread rapidly and be honoured ... And pray that we may be delivered from wicked and evil men, for not everyone has faith' (2 Thes. 3:1–2).

For our church leaders and members

'Respect those who ... are over you in the Lord ... Hold them in the highest regard in love because of their work. Live in peace with each other' (1 Thes. 5:12–13).

Monday

For the providence of God

'Oh, the depth of the riches of the wisdom and knowledge of God! How unsearchable his judgments, and his paths beyond tracing out! Who has known the mind of the Lord? Or who has been his counsellor? Who has ever given to God, that God should repay him? For from him and through him and to him are all things. To him be the glory for ever! Amen' (Rom. 11:33–36).

CONFESSION

'Do not let any unwholesome talk come out of your mouths, but only what is helpful for building others up according to their needs, that it may benefit those who listen. And do not grieve the Holy Spirit of God, with whom you were sealed for the day of redemption' (Eph. 4:29–30).

THANKSGIVING

For our home and family

'No good thing does [God] withhold from those whose walk is blameless' (Ps. 84:11).

For God's love and forgiveness

'The LORD is compassionate and gracious, slow to anger, abounding in love … He does not treat us as our sins deserve or repay us according to our iniquities. For as high as the heavens are above the earth, so great is his love for those who fear him; as far as the east is from the west, so far has he removed our transgressions from us. As a father has compassion on his children, so the LORD has compassion on those who fear him' (Ps. 103:8, 10–13).

For his Holy Spirit and the Word

'All Scripture is God-breathed and is useful for teaching, rebuking, correcting and training in righteousness, so that the man of God may be thoroughly equipped for every good work' (2 Tim. 3:16–17).

SUPPLICATION

For ourselves, our family and our church

O God who gives endurance and encouragement, give us a spirit of unity among ourselves as we follow Christ Jesus, so that with one heart and mouth we may glorify you, the God and Father of our Lord Jesus Christ. Fill us with all joy and peace as we trust in you, so that we may overflow with hope by the power of the Holy Spirit (based on Rom. 15:5–6, 13).

For true wisdom from God

'But the wisdom that comes from heaven is first of all pure; then peace-loving, considerate, submissive, full of mercy and good fruit, impartial and sincere. Peacemakers who sow in peace raise a harvest of righteousness' (James 3:17–18).

For revival

'If my people, who are called by my name, will humble themselves and pray and seek my face and turn from their wicked ways, then will I hear from heaven and will forgive their sin and will heal their land' (2 Chr. 7:14).

INTERCESSION FOR OTHERS

For persecuted Christians

'For a little while you may have had to suffer grief in all kinds of trials … so that your faith—of greater worth than gold, which perishes even though refined by fire—may be proved genuine and may result in praise, glory and honour when Jesus Christ is revealed' (1 Peter 1:6–7).

For our friends

'A friend loves at all times, and a brother is born for adversity' (Prov. 17:17).

For Christians involved in education

'A student is not above his teacher, but everyone who is fully trained will be like his teacher' (Luke 6:40).

For the moral and spiritual life of our nation

'Seek the peace and prosperity of the city to which I have carried you … Pray to the LORD for it, because if it prospers, you too will prosper' (Jer. 29:7).

Tuesday

ADORATION

For the glory of God

'All the angels were standing round the throne and around the elders and the four living creatures. They fell down on their faces before the throne and worshipped God, saying: "Amen! Praise and glory and wisdom and thanks and honour and power and strength be to our God for ever and ever. Amen!"' (Rev. 7:11–12).

For God's faithfulness

'Know therefore that the LORD your God is God; he is the faithful God, keeping his covenant of love to a thousand generations of those who love him and keep his commands' (Deut. 7:9).

CONFESSION

'I have strayed like a lost sheep. Seek your servant, for I have not forgotten your commands' (Ps. 119:176).

THANKSGIVING

For our health and God's provision of many good things

'Command those who are rich in this present world not to be arrogant nor to put their hope in wealth, which is so uncertain, but to put their hope in God, who richly provides us with everything for our enjoyment' (1 Tim. 6:17).

For assurance of salvation

'I am convinced that neither death nor life, neither angels nor demons, neither the present nor the future, nor any powers, neither height nor depth, nor anything else in all creation, will be able to separate us from the love of God that is in Christ Jesus our Lord' (Rom. 8:38–39).

SUPPLICATION

For ourselves, our family and our church

O God of our Lord Jesus Christ, our glorious Father, we pray that you will give us the Spirit of wisdom and revelation, so that we may know you better. We pray also that the eyes of our hearts may be enlightened in order that we may know the hope to which you have called us, the riches of your glorious inheritance in the saints, and your incomparably great power for us who believe (based on Eph. 1:17–19).

To be filled with the fruit of the Spirit

'The fruit of the Spirit is love, joy, peace, patience, kindness, goodness, faithfulness, gentleness and self-control … Those who belong to Christ Jesus have crucified the sinful nature with its passions and desires. Since we live by the Spirit, let us keep in step with the Spirit' (Gal. 5:22–25).

For opportunity to witness and the wise use of time

'Be very careful, then, how you live—not as unwise but as wise, making the most of every opportunity, because the days are evil' (Eph. 5:15–16).

For revival

'We have heard with our ears, O God; our fathers have told us what you did in their days, in days long ago … You have made us a reproach to our neighbours, the scorn and derision of those around us. You have made us a byword among the nations; the peoples shake their heads at us … Awake, O Lord! Why do you sleep? Rouse yourself! Do not reject us for ever. Why do you hide your face and forget our misery and oppression? … Rise up and help us; redeem us because of your unfailing love' (Ps. 44:1, 13–14, 23–24, 26).

INTERCESSION FOR OTHERS

For persecuted Christians

'Consider him who endured such opposition from sinful men, so that you will not grow weary and lose heart' (Heb. 12:3).

For Christians at work

'Whatever you do … do it all in the name of the Lord Jesus, giving thanks to God the Father through him … work at it with all your heart, as working for the Lord, not for men' (Col. 3:17, 23).

For the elderly, all who are unwell mentally or physically, and those who care for them

'Even to your old age and grey hairs I am he, I am he who will sustain you. I have made you and I will carry you; I will sustain you and I will rescue you' (Isa. 46:4).

Wednesday

ADORATION

For God's love and faithfulness

'Your love, O LORD, reaches to the heavens, your faithfulness to the skies. Your righteousness is like the mighty mountains, your justice like the great deep. O LORD, you preserve both man and beast. How priceless is your unfailing love! Both high and low among men find refuge in the shadow of your wings' (Ps. 36:5–7).

CONFESSION

'… According to your great compassion blot out my transgressions. Wash away all my iniquity and cleanse me from my sin. For I know my transgressions, and my sin is always before me. Against you, you only, have I sinned and done what is evil in your sight' (Ps. 51:1–4).

THANKSGIVING

For our home and family

'[Cornelius] and all his family were devout and God-fearing; he gave generously to those in need and prayed to God regularly' (Acts 10:2).

For freedom and peace

'The LORD is a refuge for the oppressed, a stronghold in times of trouble' (Ps. 9:9).

For the intercession of Christ

'We have a great high priest who has gone through the heavens, Jesus the Son of God … We have one who has been tempted in every way, just as we are—yet was without sin. Let us then approach the throne of grace with confidence, so that we may receive mercy and find grace to help us in our time of need' (Heb. 4:14–16).

SUPPLICATION

For ourselves, our family and our church

Lord, fill us with the knowledge of your will through all spiritual wisdom and understanding, in order that we may live lives worthy of you and may please you in every way. Help us to bear fruit in every good work and to grow in the knowledge of God. Strengthen us with all power according to your glorious might so that we may have great endurance and patience, and joyfully give thanks to you, who have qualified us to share in the inheritance of the saints in the kingdom of light (based on Col. 1:9–12).

To be strong in Christ

'Be strong in the Lord and in his mighty power. Put on the full armour of God so that you can take your stand against the devil's schemes … And pray in the Spirit on all occasions with all kinds of prayers and requests. With this in mind, be alert and always keep on praying for all the saints' (Eph. 6:10–11, 18).

For revival

'"Has God forgotten to be merciful? Has he in anger withheld his compassion?" Then I thought, "To this I will appeal: the years of the right hand of the Most High." I will remember the deeds of the LORD; yes, I will remember your miracles of long ago. I will meditate on all your works and consider all your mighty deeds. Your ways, O God, are holy. What god is so great as our God? You are the God who performs miracles; you display your power among the peoples' (Ps. 77:9–14).

INTERCESSION FOR OTHERS

For persecuted Christians

'Consider it pure joy, my brothers, whenever you face trials of many kinds, because you know that the testing of your faith develops perseverance' (James 1:2–3).

For singles and those bereaved

'If you have any encouragement from being united with Christ, if any comfort from his love, if any fellowship with the Spirit, if any tenderness and compassion, then make my joy complete by being like-minded, having the same love, being one in spirit and purpose' (Phil. 2:1–2).

For housewives and mothers

'Train a child in the way he should go, and when he is old he will not turn from it' (Prov. 22:6).

Thursday

ADORATION

The Triune God and his electing love

'[You have been] chosen according to the foreknowledge of God the Father, through the sanctifying work of the Spirit, for obedience to Jesus Christ and sprinkling by his blood … Praise be to the God and Father of our Lord Jesus Christ! In his great mercy he has given us new birth into a living hope through the resurrection of Jesus Christ from the dead, and into an inheritance that can never perish, spoil or fade—kept in heaven for you' (1 Peter 1:2–4).

CONFESSION

'He who conceals his sins does not prosper, but whoever confesses and renounces them finds mercy' (Prov. 28:13; see also 6:16–19).

THANKSGIVING

For the privilege of being a Christian

'To all who received him, to those who believed in his name, he gave the right to become children of God' (John 1:12).

For God's promises

'Through [God's goodness and glory] he has given us his very great and precious promises, so that through them you may participate in the divine nature and escape the corruption in the world caused by evil desires' (2 Peter 1: 4).

For the certain hope of Christ's return

'… We wait for the blessed hope—the glorious appearing of our great God and Saviour, Jesus Christ' (Titus 2:13).

SUPPLICATION

For ourselves, our family and our church

Lord, we pray that you may count us worthy of your calling, and that by your power you will fulfil every good purpose of ours and every act prompted by our faith. We pray this so that the name of our Lord Jesus may be glorified in us, and we in him, according to the grace of our God and the Lord Jesus Christ (based on 2 Thes. 1:11–12).

To be kept pure

'For God did not call us to be impure, but to live a holy life' (1 Thes. 4:7).

To be humble in assessing others

'So then, each of us will give an account of himself to God. Therefore let us stop passing judgment on one another. Instead, make up your mind not to put any stumbling-block or obstacle in your brother's way' (Rom. 14:12–13).

For revival

'Restore us again, O God our Saviour, and put away your displeasure towards us. Will you be angry with us for ever? Will you prolong your anger through all generations? Will you not revive us again, that your people may rejoice in you? Show us your unfailing love, O LORD, and grant us your salvation … The LORD will indeed give what is good, and our land will yield its harvest. Righteousness goes before him and prepares the way for his steps' (Ps. 85:4–7, 12–13).

INTERCESSION FOR OTHERS

For persecuted Christians

'If you suffer as a Christian, do not be ashamed, but praise God that you bear that name' (1 Peter 4:16).

For unsaved relatives, friends, neighbours and colleagues

'The Lord is … patient with you, not wanting anyone to perish, but everyone to come to repentance' (2 Peter 3:9).

For those in the police and security forces

'He has delivered us from such a deadly peril, and he will deliver us. On him we have set our hope that he will continue to deliver us' (2 Cor. 1:10).

Friday

ADORATION

For the power of God

'Sing to God, O kingdoms of the earth, sing praise to the Lord, to him who rides the ancient skies above, who thunders with mighty voice. Proclaim the power of God, whose majesty is over Israel, whose power is in the skies. You are awesome, O God, in your sanctuary; the God of Israel gives power and strength to his people. Praise be to God!' (Ps. 68:32–35).

For the presence of God

'O LORD, you have searched me and you know me. You know when I sit and when I rise; you perceive my thoughts from afar. You discern my going out and my lying down; you are familiar with all my ways. Before a word is on my tongue you know it completely, O LORD. You hem me in—behind and before; you have laid your hand upon me. Such knowledge is too wonderful for me, too lofty for me to attain. Where can I go from your Spirit? Where can I flee from your presence?' (Ps. 139:1–7).

CONFESSION

'But if you harbour bitter envy and selfish ambition in your hearts, do not boast about it or deny the truth. Such "wisdom" does not come down from heaven but is earthly, unspiritual, of the devil. For where you have envy and selfish ambition, there you find disorder and every evil practice' (James 3:14–16).

THANKSGIVING

For our home and family

'... Rejoice in all the good things the LORD your God has given to you and your household' (Deut. 26:11).

For the peace of God

'... And the peace of God, which transcends all understanding, will guard your hearts and your minds in Christ Jesus' (Phil. 4:7).

For the love of God

'How great is the love the Father has lavished on us, that we should be called children of God!' (1 John 3:1).

SUPPLICATION

For ourselves, our family and our church

Lord, may our love abound more and more in knowledge and depth of insight, so that we may be able to discern what is best and may be pure and blameless until the day of Christ, filled with the fruit of righteousness that comes through Jesus Christ, to your glory and praise (based on Phil. 1:9–11).

To cultivate a Christian character

'Make every effort to add to your faith goodness; and to goodness, knowledge; and to knowledge, self-control; and to self-control, perseverance; and to perseverance, godliness; and to godliness, brotherly kindness; and to brotherly kindness, love' (2 Peter 1:5–7).

For revival

'Oh, that you would rend the heavens and come down … to make your name known to your enemies and cause the nations to quake before you! … Since ancient times no one has heard, no ear has perceived, no eye has seen any God besides you, who acts on behalf of those who wait for him. You come to the help of those who gladly do right, who remember your ways' (Isa. 64:1–2, 4–5).

INTERCESSION FOR OTHERS

For persecuted Christians

'Those who suffer according to God's will should commit themselves to their faithful Creator and continue to do good' (1 Peter 4:19).

For evangelism across the nation

'Devote yourselves to prayer, being watchful and thankful … that God may open a door for our message' (Col. 4:2–3).

For leaders in national and local government

'I urge, then, first of all, that requests, prayers, intercession and thanksgiving be made for everyone—for kings and all those in authority, that we may live peaceful and quiet lives in all godliness and holiness' (1 Tim. 2:1–2).

Saturday

ADORATION

For the holiness of God

'I saw the Lord seated on a throne, high and exalted, and the train of his robe filled the temple. Above him were seraphs, each with six wings: With two wings they covered their faces, with two they covered their feet, and with two they were flying. And they were calling to one another: "Holy, holy, holy is the LORD Almighty; the whole earth is full of his glory" ' (Isa. 6:1–3).

CONFESSION

'You have set our iniquities before you, our secret sins in the light of your presence' (Ps. 90:8).

THANKSGIVING

For the Word of God

'Your word is a lamp to my feet and a light for my path' (Ps. 119:105).

For the hope of heaven

'... We wait for the blessed hope—the glorious appearing of our great God and Saviour, Jesus Christ' (Titus 2:13).

For the universal and local church

'All over the world this gospel is bearing fruit and growing' (Col. 1:6).

SUPPLICATION

For ourselves, our family and our church

May you yourself, the God of peace, sanctify us through and through. May our whole spirit, soul and body be kept blameless at the coming of our Lord Jesus Christ (based on 1 Thes. 5:23).

To be wise and generous in giving

'Give, and it will be given to you. A good measure, pressed down, shaken together and running over, will be poured into your lap. For with the measure you use, it will be measured to you' (Luke 6:38).

For revival

'I will pour water on the thirsty land, and streams on the dry ground; I will pour out my Spirit on your offspring, and my blessing on your descendants. They will spring up like grass in a meadow, like poplar trees by flowing streams. One will say, "I belong to the LORD"; another will call himself by the name of Jacob; still another will write on his hand, "The LORD's", and will take the name Israel' (Isa. 44:3–5).

INTERCESSION FOR OTHERS

For persecuted Christians

'When you pass through the waters, I will be with you … When you walk through the fire, you will not be burned; the flames will not set you ablaze. For I am the LORD, your God, the Holy One of Israel, your Saviour' (Isa. 43:2–3).

For evangelism in prisons across our country

'If anyone is in Christ, he is a new creation; the old has gone, the new has come! All this is from God, who reconciled us to himself through Christ and gave us the ministry of reconciliation' (2 Cor. 5:17–18).

For churches known to us

'I will build my church, and the gates of Hades will not overcome it' (Matt. 16:18).

For those preparing for ministry

'Pray for us … that we may proclaim the mystery of Christ … clearly', 'in truthful speech and in the power of God' (Col. 4:3–4; 2 Cor. 6:7).

EVIDENCE for the BIBLE

Clive Anderson and
Brian Edwards

LARGE FORMAT HARDBACK
FULL COLOUR THROUGHOUT
225mm × 275mm
260pp | ISBN 978-1-84625-416-1
REF EFB4161 | £25.00

EVIDENCE
for the BIBLE

Clive Anderson and Brian Edwards   Day One

Evidence will surprise and inform you as you turn over the soil of history with the pages of your Bible. The witness of the trowel authenticates and illuminates the people and events, lifting them from the pages of the Book and setting them in the context of time and place. Join us on an exciting journey with this evidence from the past.

Evidence for the Bible can be found in many places, from the Ancient Near East to museums and private collections. Whilst artefacts can never prove the authority of the Bible, they can and do show that the events described in the Bible occurred in time and history.

This book provides a selection of the many items that demonstrate the reliability of the Bible as a historical document.

'Clive Anderson and Brian Edwards have captured the essence of generations of middle-eastern archaeology, historical context and biblical landscape in a quite remarkable way. Their book is accessible, informative and enjoyable. The pictures beautifully complement the text. The Bible comes alive. I warmly and wholeheartedly commend it to everyone who wishes to be a little wiser and better informed about the Book which has formed our culture and is the source of the Christian Faith.'
THE VERY REVD JAMES ATWELL,
Dean of Winchester.

'This is a marvellous introduction to the finds of archaeology that illumine our understanding of the Bible. It helps the reader to see that the biblical events and writings took place within history. When the reader studies the Bible, this book will serve as a wonderful tool to help get at its depth and richness. I highly recommend it.'
DR JOHN D CURRID
Carl McMurray Professor of Old Testament at the Reformed Theological Seminary, Charlotte, USA.